N Scale Model Railroad That Grows

Step-by-step instructions for building your first N scale layout

KENT WOOD AND RIC LABAN

KALMBACH BOOKS

Printed in the United States of America

Publisher's Cataloging in Publication
(Prepared by Quality Books Inc.)

Wood, Kent.
 N scale model railroad that grows / Kent Wood and Ric LaBan.
 p. cm.
 Includes index.
 ISBN 0-89024-223-2

 1. Railroads—Models. I. LaBan, Ric. II. Title.

TF197.W66 1996   625.1'9
                                    QBI96-20275

Cover design: Kristi Ludwig
Book design: Mark Watson

Contents

Fig. 1. This photo captures the action of an SP Consolidation as it crosses the North American lake.

The Great N-pire Railroad, a Miniature Model Railroad You Can Build

WELCOME to the enjoyable hobby of N scale model railroading. The object of this book is to teach you how to build your first model railroad. Following the step-by-step instructions provided in this book, you'll learn how to build your first model railroad, the Great N-pire Railroad.

Perhaps you received a train set for Christmas, and you want to use it for a permanent layout. Maybe you had a model railroad while you were growing up, gave it up, and are now interested in getting back into the hobby. Or maybe you've always been fascinated by miniatures, dioramas, or model railroading and just didn't know where to start. We congratulate you on taking the first step into a miniature world, for whatever reason. Like you, thousands of people have found N scale model railroading to be one of the most enjoyable, relaxing, and rewarding hobbies around.

The Great N-pire Railroad is not a difficult layout to build. You don't need any prior model-building experience to complete any project, nor you do have to be an artist; all you need is the willingness to roll up your sleeves and try it.

You'll use simple hand and hobby tools to build your railroad in sections, one at a time. The only "power" tools you need are an electric soldering gun and a hot glue gun. The materials for building the Great N-pire Railroad are easy to obtain from art, craft, construction supply, and hobby stores. Other model railroading books by Kalmbach Publishing Co., *Model Railroader* magazine, your local hobby store, and fellow model railroaders are excellent additional resources.

Design of the Great N-pire Railroad

N scale model railroading refers to two different things: scale, in this case, a ratio of 160 scale feet to 1 actual foot; and track gauge, the distance between the rails, which equals nine millimeters—hence the name "N." Nine millimeters is approximately ⅜", making a 40-foot boxcar equal to 3 inches. That is quite small for an operating railroad.

N scale's small size was the primary design element of the Great

Fig. 2. In N scale there are 160 scale feet to 1 real foot. This proportion makes a 40-foot N scale boxcar 3 inches long. N scale derives its name from the width of its track, which is nine millimeters. Such a small size is an asset, because more railroading can be packed into a smaller space.

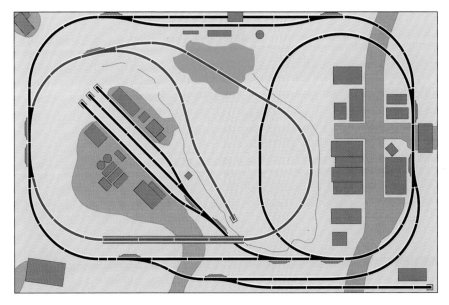

Fig. 3. This is the final stage of the Great N-pire Railroad as shown in a computer-aided design (CAD) drawing of the track plan.

N-pire Railroad. You can build a 40" x 60" railroad with a great amount of railroad action and detail in a short time just because of size. You can construct the tabletop base alone in the course of an afternoon. A tabletop layout also saves time by not requiring additional benchwork.

The Great N-pire Railroad's greatest asset is its "growing"

track plan. We start with a simple oval of track—little more than what comes in a prepackaged train set—and build it into a more sophisticated and attractive layout through each successive expansion. This evolving design means you can stop at any point after the initial phase and still have an operating layout that is complete with trackwork,

Figs. 4 and 5. These two illustrations demonstrate different landscaping ideas for the Great N-pire Railroad, while still using the same track plan. One illustration (upper) is based on the concept developed in this book, while the other (lower) is a more industrialized urban layout. The drawings are courtesy of our good friend and fellow model railroader, Art Tom.

structures, and scenery!

In the first stage you'll build a simple track loop with a two-track industrial yard and some basic scenery. Track expansion begins in the second phase; it adds a third industrial yard spur and a steam or passing siding. In the third phase you'll add another passing siding, a freight spur, and an interior oval known as the Shortline. In the fourth and last expansion phase the elevated Highline and mine spur finish the layout. This is the Great N-pire Railroad in all its glory, ready to haul freight from one end of the country to another—across mountains, through tunnels, to the valleys below. But the most exciting aspect of building the Great N-pire Railroad is that you can create your own version, using your talent and imagination!

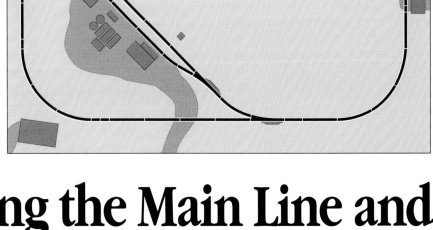

Fig. 1-1. A layout consists of a train-board with a track plan, scenery, and structures on which engines and rolling stock operate. This is the basic layout that you'll build in this section.

Building the Main Line and Industrial Switching Yard

REAL RAILROADS use the earth beneath the tracks as their support. Our Great N-pire Railroad also requires a solid foundation. A well-constructed trainboard provides the frame on which our railroad will grow (fig. 1-1). Our construction technique will be fast, simple but sturdy, lightweight, and easily transportable. In fact, if you use a hot glue gun and spray adhesive, and follow the method we present, you can complete the project in only a few hours!

Most model railroads were traditionally built with lumber benchwork and covered by plywood or Homasote. While there is nothing wrong with using these materials for this project, the resulting

7

Fig. 1-2. Here are the tools and supplies listed in Table 1 that you'll need to build the foam-core trainboard base.

layout would be rock-solid but overengineered and heavy.

We chose foam core for our construction material. Used by artists, sign makers, architectural model builders, and photographers, foam core is a rigid lightweight board that cuts easily with a hobby or utility knife. You can find it at art supply stores, hobby and craft shops, photographic processing labs, or frame shops where they laminate and mount photos or artwork.

Foam core comes in a variety of thicknesses, sizes, and colors. We based the 40" x 60" width and length of the layout on the largest size foam core that was readily available. If you can't find a large ½"-thick sheet, or if it is more expensive than two ³⁄₁₆" sheets, you can laminate two sheets of ³⁄₁₆" together to make a sheet approximately ½" thick. Spray adhesive, yellow carpenter's glue, or contact cement are good glues to use for laminating.

Remember, if a specific material or size is not readily available in your area, make an appropriate substitution. There's always more than one way to accomplish a given task or effect. It is more important to keep the railroad moving toward completion than to hold out for a certain product.

We highly recommend using a hot glue gun (a model rated at 80

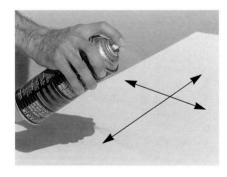

Fig. 1-3. A ½"-thick sheet of 40" x 60" foam core was unavailable, so we laminated two ³⁄₁₆"-thick sheets with overlapping strokes of spray adhesive.

Fig. 1-4a. This is the pattern for cutting the braces, joists, sides, and ends from a foam-core sheet.

	40"		
	Extra		
2"	9½"	9½"	9½"
2"	9½"	9½"	9½"
2"	39"		
2"	39"		
2"	39"		
2"	39"		
2"	39"		
2"	39"		
2"	39"		
2"	20"		20"
2"	40"		
2"	40"		

32"

Fig. 1-5. Cut the foam-core framing strips with a steel rule and X-acto knife. A sheet of cardboard protects the tabletop from scratches.

Fig. 1-6. Mark the underside of the laminated tabletop according to the framing pattern in fig. 1-4b and use the lines as guides for joists and center stringer braces.

watts or higher) for many parts of this project. We use a glue gun for construction, laying roadbed, building scenery, and everything else imaginable. Please read the manufacturer's instructions and warnings carefully before you use the gun. Hot glue guns are marvelous tools, but as with any tool, safety comes first. Elmer's yellow carpenter's glue is a readily available alternative adhesives for lamination and construction. If you use it you need some type of weight—such as heavy books—to hold the pieces together until the glue dries. Use only yellow glue; white glue shrinks and can warp the material. This glue method is time tested and reliable, but it takes time for the glue to dry completely before you can add bracing. After it dries for a day, you can start the next phase of construction. Now, assemble the materials in Table 1-2, roll up your sleeves, and get to work!

First, you'll laminate a foam-core tabletop, if necessary. Then you'll mark, cut, and glue the foam-core sides, ends, joists, and stringer braces. If you were able to find a single 1/2" x 40" x 60" sheet of foam core for your table-top, you are ready to mark, cut, and glue the framed base. If you could find only 3/16" sheets, you'll need to laminate them together. We prefer Scotch brand spray adhesive 77 over the other spray adhesives because it is more powerful and won't debond when used on paper. You'll want to spray outside on a calm day or in a large space like a garage or basement floor. Cover your work area with newspapers to catch the overspray, or you will have a sticky floor. Most important, read and follow the instructions on the back of the can (fig. 1-3). Spray both surfaces, or the sheets will delaminate.

Figures 1-4a and 1-4b show you the cutting and assembly pattern you'll use for the trainboard sides, ends, joists, and center stringer braces. Measure, mark, and cut the 1/2" x 32" x 40" foam core into twelve 2"-wide, 40"-long strips (fig.1-5). From these twelve strips you will then cut shorter lengths. You'll need a total of two 40" strips, two 20" strips, seven 39" strips, and six 9½" strips. With either an X-acto knife or a utility knife, use several light strokes rather than a single heavy cut to stroke through the foam core. A single stroke of the knife will only tear, rip, and gouge the

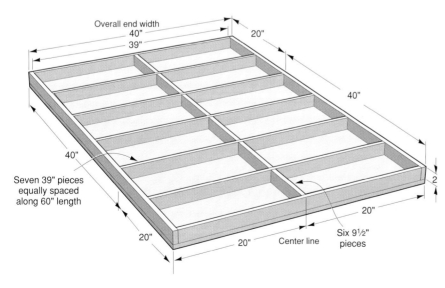

Fig. 1-4b. This is the framing pattern of the 40" x 60" trainboard. Note the staggered side pieces.

Fig. 1-7. A machinist's square keeps the sides square while the hot-glue gun fastens them together with a bead of hot glue.

Fig. 1-8. Glue the tabletop sides along the corner's vertical seams as well.

foam core. Number each strip, either consecutively or by length, so it will be glued in its correct place and in the proper sequence.

Choose one surface of the tabletop to be the underside and mark a center line, at 20" lengthwise down the middle of the board. This is the reference line for stringer braces. Next mark the board from side to side every 10" along the 60" length from one end to the other. These become the reference lines for the joists (fig. 1-6). Match and number the corresponding reference lines to the numbered strips.

Once the tabletop is ready, fire up the glue gun and finish assembling the trainboard by gluing the framed base to the tabletop. First,

glue the exterior sides around the board's perimeter, starting with a 60" side. The 60" sides are comprised of two foam-core pieces each: a 40"-long, 2"-wide strip, butted and glued end to end with a 20"-long, 2"-wide strip. Notice in fig. 1-4b that the butt-joints of these two side pieces are staggered and reversed from one side to the other for additional support. Start at one corner, and use a square to keep the sides perpendicular to the tabletop while gluing along just the interior seam (fig. 1-7). Unlike white glue, applied between the pieces, hot glue has more than enough strength to hold when applied along all the interior seams. Follow the first side by gluing a

39" end. Use the square as shown in fig. 1-7, then glue both the vertical interior seams (fig. 1-8). Continue around the perimeter until all the pieces are glued into place. Glue the remaining five 39" interior joists on the center of the scribed lines that are 10" apart (fig. 1-4b). Finally glue the six 9½" interior stringer braces, centered, on the scribed 20" midline. Once all the pieces are glued together, you'll want to cover all exterior side seams with scotch tape. This will provide a smooth surface when you paint the sides later (fig. 1-9).

Congratulations, you now have (don't tell Columbus) a flat rectangular terra firma on which to construct the Great N-pire

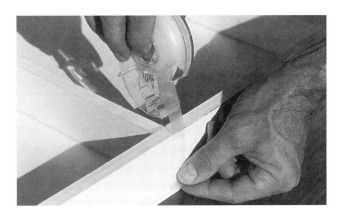

Fig. 1-9. Cover and hide the side seams with cellophane tape before painting.

Fig. 1-11. Mark the trackwork starting at a point 12" from the west end and 1" from the north side.

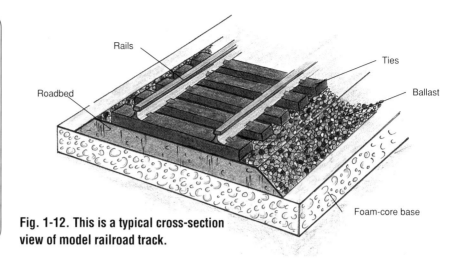

Fig. 1-12. This is a typical cross-section view of model railroad track.

Railroad. This was easy, wasn't it? No other part of building the Great N-pire Railroad is any more difficult than this—and most of it is even more fun!

Laying Out the Track Plan

You have now constructed the trainboard upon which the Great N-pire will grow. Now you'll survey your route, lay out the Main-line track plan (hence the term "layout"), put down roadbed, wire the layout for operation, build some basic scenery, and assemble the first industry and trackside structures. Then you can put on an engineer's hat, pick up your train orders, and open up the throttle.

Gather the materials listed in Table 1-2 so you can survey the route and proceed to lay track.

Choose one of the longer sides to be north, marking it with an N (fig. 1-10). Mark the other long side with an S for south; the appropriate ends are east and west.

You'll have to do some preliminary work along the west edge of the trainboard before laying out the track plan. Use a 12" x 40" sheet of ½"-thick foam core to

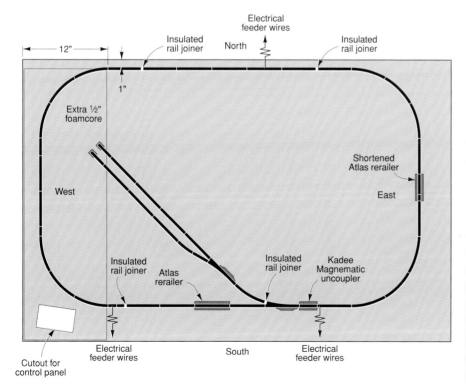

Fig. 1-10. The computer-aided design (CAD) track plan includes all the important dimensions and data.

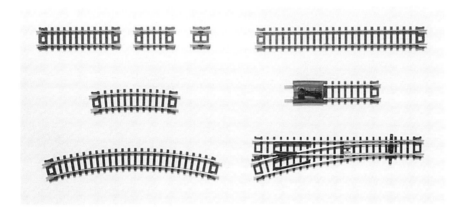

Fig. 1-13. We used these standard Atlas track sections during the construction of our layout.

build the foundation for the scenic bluffs. This is the first step to making the trainboard look more like rolling countryside than like an empty parking lot. Temporarily fasten the foam core in place with push pins.

The north side is the key to laying out the track plan. Notice that the oval is offset toward the northwest corner, allowing all the trackwork to fit within the confines of the trainboard—you don't want one of your trains falling off the edge of the earth! With a tape measure and sharpened pencil in hand, you can begin laying out the track plan

by marking a starting point 12" in from the west end (along the north side) and 1" in from the north edge (fig. 1-11). Draw this line all the way to the east end of the tabletop. This is the guideline for the first straight section. It's time now for the ties, rails, and spikes listed in Table 1-3.

On a real railroad the trackwork is made up of several different elements, starting with steel rails that are spiked to wooden crossbars, known as ties (fig. 1-12). Spikes hold the rails in place on the ties. Roadbed, a berm of graded earth, elevates track above the surrounding ground.

Ballast, a layer of cinders, crushed rock, or gravel, is packed on top of the roadbed and between the ties to hold the track in place and to hasten water drainage. N gauge track, on the other hand, is a fabrication of conductive metal rails and plastic ties, available in different lengths and configurations.

In model railroading you use 36" lengths of prefashioned roadbed made out of pressed cork. Ballast is finely ground rock or synthetic material. After you transfer the layout plan to the trainboard, you'll glue roadbed onto the track plan, secure the track to the roadbed with nails or glue, wire the track, and finish it with scale ballast.

As we began our trackwork, we found that Atlas sectional track gave us pleasing results. Atlas track offers several advantages for a first railroad—most hobby shops carry it, assembly is easy, and all the sections are standardized (fig. 1-13). Other companies make equally fine track, but the length of the sections may be different from that of Atlas track (fig. 1-14). Our track foreman substituted a single piece of

Fig. 1-14. Different manufacturers may produce different lengths of straight sections. A Bachmann straight section, above, is shorter than the comparable Atlas straight section, below. Use only one manufacturer's brand of track for consistent lengths.

Fig. 1-15. Pin the first straight section of track in place at the starting point marked in fig. 1-11.

Bachmann straight track on one side of the oval during the track-laying. After everything was glued in place we discovered that our oval was short on one side! If you decide to use another brand of track, be sure to use equal numbers of the same pieces on each side.

Select seven pieces of 5" straight track from the list in Table 1-3 and start laying out the track plan. Refer to fig. 1-10 for the correct number of track sections and the sequence. Begin laying track by pinning the first straight section at the starting point as shown in fig. 1-15. Push each section together snugly, using rail joiners on each rail between the sections. One push pin per length will hold each track section in place. Continue laying straight track east until you have laid all seven sections along the guideline.

Create the first curve by connecting three curved sections end to end. Three 9¾"-radius curved sections make a complete 90-degree turn. The first turn should bring the track's outer tie edge approximately 4½" from the east end. Following the track plan precisely, lay the pieces in the following order: a 5" straight section, a 2½" piece, a 1⅝" piece, and finally another 5" straight. The reason behind this and other unusual configurations will become apparent in future expansions. In this case, you will replace the 5" sections with switches for the passing track and Shortline. Now, pin down three more curved sections, and you'll have laid half the oval.

After the second curve, the track's outer edge should be 5¼" from the south edge. If you draw a line along the south side as you did on the north side, you'll have a reference line to keep this

Fig. 1-16. Both of these track switches are made by Atlas. We prefer the Custom Line version, above, with a Caboose Industries' ground throw instead of the lower version, which has an unrealistic 40-scale-foot switch machine. Do not install the ground throw now.

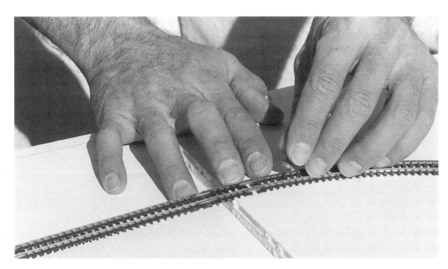

Fig. 1-17. As the track climbs the additional ½"-thick section of foam core (the base for the Indian Bluffs), pin the main line's third triplet of curves in place.

straightaway parallel to the train-board edge. The first piece laid after the curve is a 5" straight piece. Follow it by a 2½" straight, which will hold a Kadee uncoupling magnet. (Later, we'll show you how to install the magnet in this short section.)

A right-hand switch comes next. A switch is a piece of track that diverts a train from one track to another. Model railroaders also call switches "turnouts" so they

can't be confused with the electrical switches that route electricity. Throughout this book we will always use the term "electrical switch" to denote any switch having to do with electricity or electronics.

We recommend using Atlas Custom Line switches (fig. 1-16). These switches are designed by the Atlas Tool Company for reliable operation. The older versions are still available, so make

Fig. 1-18. The upper, untreated section of track appears toylike compared to the track below after its painting treatment. After completing all tracklaying, add the ballast, which further enhances the realistic appearance.

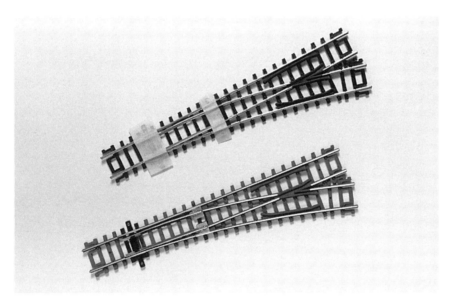

Fig. 1-19. Protect all track switch contact points with tape before spray-painting. Afterward, you can do touch-up painting on the rails and ties by brush.

sure you buy the Custom Line. We purchased ours without a manual or electric switch machine because we prefer to use Caboose Industries no. 206S ground throws. They provide positive mechanical action and realistic operation.

The Atlas switch machines are long (40 scale feet) and difficult to disguise. The smaller overall size of the Great N-pire means

that you can't use electric switch machines, with one exception in the final stage of expansion. If you want all electric switch machines, or if you want to convert this one now, read ahead in the wiring explanation.

After the right-hand switch, lay another 5" straight section, the Atlas rerailer, and another 5" straight piece. At this point you'll have to add two small track

sections to the length of the southside straightaway to equal the northside's seven straight sections. The advantage of Atlas sectional track is that a 2½" section plus a 1¼" section and a ⅝" section equals one piece of standard straight track. You used the 2½" section before the switch, so you now need one 1¼" section and a ⅝" piece to complete this side.

You'll now lay the third curve in the oval. This is also where you placed the additional ½"-thick sheet of foam core to raise the height of the track. Eventually the Highline's track starts its climb from this elevation. Pin the three curved 9¾"-radius sections as you did on the other end (fig. 1-17). You'll need to match the length of the straight sections at the east end. The first straight piece is a 1¼". Follow it by two standard sections, then the 2½" part. Three more curves will complete the mainline oval. If there is a slight misalignment, check all the track, pull up a few push pins, and realign the track to fit. The rail joiners should hold all sections together tightly.

A switching yard to service industry is the last track group that you lay out in this stage. The yard entrance begins at the turnout side of the southside switch. Substitute a 9¾"-radius curved section for the curved section that comes in every switch package. The 9¾" curve here properly aligns the industrial switching yard to the rest of the layout (fig. 1-10). The curved track that comes with the switch is designed to create a parallel track from the switch's turnout to the mainline. We'll use these extra curves in the next chapter.

After installing the first switch and curve section, install a left-handed Custom Line switch. The spur (a length of track that dead-ends) from the this switch consists of four 5" straight pieces and an Atlas bumper section. The turnout side of the switch uses a 2½" straight piece followed by a half curved section. This track combination will give you room for a switch machine (Atlas brand) between the industrial spurs. Add three more 5" straight sections and an Atlas bumper section to the turnout side. Both yard spurs should be parallel and equal in length at the bumper's end. Secure each piece in place with a push pin, and you are finished laying out the track plan.

Painting the Track

You'll achieve the illusion of realism in the Great N-pire model railroad by paying close attention to little details. Many of these details are not difficult to accomplish. They may require a little time, but they are well worth the effort. Right from the package, track has a plastic, toylike look. A sprayed coat of Floquil rail brown spray paint and fine ballast helps create the weathered realism of real track. Figure 1-18 illustrates how to build realistic track in stages. Don't ballast the trackage until you have completed all the expansion stages. Tearing up

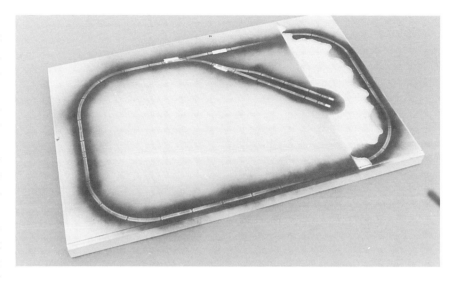

Fig. 1-20. This is the track pattern left on the tabletop after spray-painting and removing the pinned track. Use this pattern for gluing the cork roadbed in place.

secured and ballasted track for expansion is difficult to do without damaging it.

Protective eyeglasses and a dust mask are the minimal precautions to take while you're spray-painting. Another good precaution is to use some type of gloves. Spray aerosols create a poisonous mist that can be dangerous. The microscopic particles are easily inhaled into the lungs where they are quickly absorbed by the blood and deposited in the organs. Absorption can even occur through the skin, a wet trigger finger, or the membranes of the eyeball! Long-term exposure can create toxic levels in your body that endanger your health. Please don't risk

your health. We want you to have many happy times with your railroad.

Before you start spray-painting, cover the electrical contact points of the switches with masking tape. Figure 1-19 shows before and after photos of the protected contact points. Do not spray-paint the switches without taking this precaution! We did, and we ruined a switch—it would not pass current because the paint insulated the contact points. You can touch up the outer brass rail edges with a brush afterward.

Spray from both sides and both ends to cover all track surfaces. Broad, even strokes from all directions are more effective than short staccato bursts. Continue

Fig. 1-21. This illustration shows the transformation of scenery stage by stage. Using our step-by-step techniques, you'll progress from barren terrain to finished presentation.

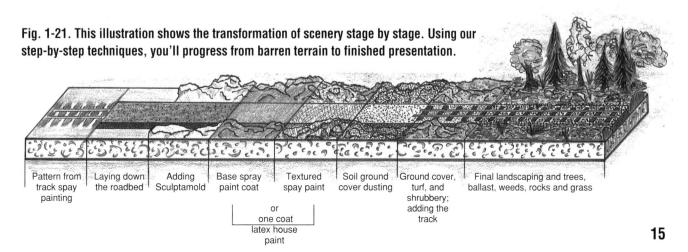

Pattern from track spay painting | Laying down the roadbed | Adding Sculptamold | Base spray paint coat | Textured spay paint | Soil ground cover dusting | Ground cover, turf, and shrubbery; adding the track | Final landscaping and trees, ballast, weeds, rocks and grass

or one coat latex house paint

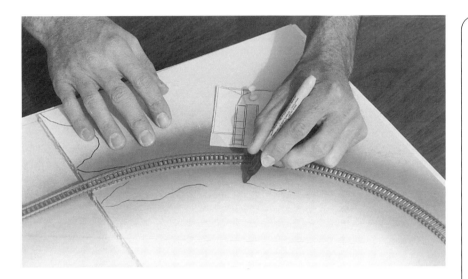

Fig. 1-22. Before cutting, draw the rough shape of the bluffs around the track pattern on the extra foam-core sheet.

Table 1-4. Supply List

- Amaco Sculptamold and water for mixing
- Bowl and putty knife
- Paper towels for cleanup
- X-acto knife
- Hot glue gun and glue sticks
- 6 pieces of N scale cork roadbed
- Flat tan (or base tint) latex house paint or
- 1 can Krylon spray paint no. 2412 light peach, and
- 1 kit Plasti-Kote Fleckstone
- spray paint no. 438 canyon rock
- A contrasting color for trainboard sides
- 18' wood corner molding
- 17' ½" flat wood molding
- Saw and miter box to cut molding (or use the one at the store)

spraying around the track plan until all the track is covered. You'll clean the rail tops after securing them with track nails to the roadbed. Now, once the paint has dried, remove the track from the trainboard. Surprise! You now have a pattern to use as a roadbed and shaping template (fig. 1-20).

Roadbed and Basic Scenery Techniques

Many modelers consider scenery the most enjoyable part of model railroading. The transformation from empty shell to a miniature world is astonishing (fig. 1-21). You do not have to be an artist to create good-looking scenery, so don't let it scare you. Building scenery is simpler than you think with our proven methods. Step by step we'll help you achieve results that are both spectacular and breathtaking. You'll begin with basic but effective techniques and build upon that knowledge to more elaborate constructions. There's just one rule to building scenery—if you don't like what you construct, just tear it up and start over!

Trains travel across the land through scenery for a reason. Ask yourself some questions. Why does my railroad exist? What does it do to generate revenue? Where is it located geographically? Answers to these questions will clarify the type of scenery you will build. Our Western American

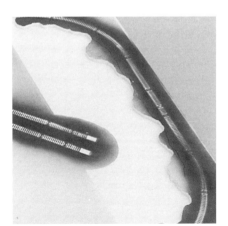

Fig. 1-23. Even though this land form is roughly symmetrical, strive for an irregular outline of bluffs.

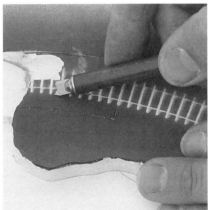

Fig. 1-24. Cut through the foam core at an angle with an X-acto knife to create a ramp for easing the track from one level of foam core to another.

Fig. 1-25. Sculptamold sculpted with a putty knife completes the grading transition from tabletop to bluff.

Fig. 1-26. A pair of Southern Pacific F7s have plenty of side clearance to move a freight train through the Indian Bluffs.

Fig. 1-27. Separate the cork roadbed halves by pulling them apart. The inner sides become the outer sides when the roadbed is glued to the tabletop.

version of the Great N-pire Railroad exists primarily because of mining. This setting gives us the opportunity to model what we like: mountains, canyons, mesas, water, trestles, etc.

In the Introduction you saw two conceptual illustrations of how the same Great N-pire layout would look in two different geographic locations. You can build the rugged western landscape illustrated—or you may choose to sculpt the terrain of your own geographic locale. Allow your imagination to run wild. Incorporating your favorite scenes within the Great N-pire Railroad adds a distinctive personal touch

that makes it yours alone. Once you decide on the setting for your railroad, study the location first hand or through reference photographs, so you can model the shape, texture, and color of any subject.

Sculpting Indian Bluffs with Sculptamold

Indian Bluffs, named by nervous settlers who watched smoke signals emanate from the bluffs, are created from the extra sheet of foam core on the west end. Figures 1-22 and 1-23 illustrate the irregular horseshoe shape of the foam-core hill. Since the

bluffs are elevated, the roadbed and track require a subroadbed ramp from the tabletop to the new height. First, cut into the sheet around the track pattern and use a sliver of 1/4"-thick foam core (left over from building the trainboard) as a transition between heights (fig. 1-24). Then glue the bluff sheet to the trainboard.

You'll finish the ramps using a product called Sculptamold (see Table 1-4). Sculptamold, a papier-maché-like compound made of cellulose, is a favorite among model railroaders. Mix it in small batches according to the manufacturer's directions. Use a putty

Fig. 1-28. Hold the inside half of the roadbed in place until the hot glue sets. If you use a different type of glue, push pins will keep the roadbed in place until the glue sets.

Fig. 1-29. Lay down a second bead of glue for the outer half of the roadbed, and glue it in the same manner.

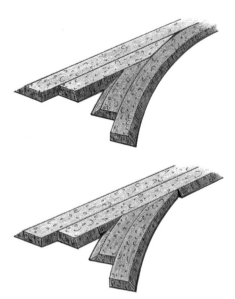

Fig. 1-30. Track switches require a roadbed pattern from two sections of roadbed. Use the upper pattern for the main line when you're first laying track. Use the pattern below for the expansion phases, when you're adding switches to existing trackwork.

Fig. 1-31. Use an overlap cut to match the ends of the roadbed when completing the mainline oval.

knife to apply the compound and level the unfinished ramps (fig. 1-25).

Now work your way across the west end, varying the shapes and slopes of the mounds and bluffs. Be sure to allow ample clearance for the roadbed, track, and locomotives along the sides of the bluffs (fig. 1-26). Don't forget to leave a level area in the southwest corner for the control panel. Also, the area on the inside of the straight section should be reasonably level for the switches and the Highline Oval in the last expansion phase.

Relax and take your time forming the bluffs. Avoid having too many look-alike shapes, and vary the heights. We made the bluffs higher and higher as we moved across the west end. You can always change the shapes if you are not satisfied. When you've finished modeling the Sculpta-mold, you'll be surprised at how easy it was to create shape. The addition of color and texture will enhance the landscape.

Laying Down the Roadbed

Cork roadbed provides a support for the track and a noise dampener for the electric train engines. It also produces a realistic slope for ballast. You'll start laying strips on the southwest curve where the control panel will go. A hot glue gun shortens the process, but yellow glue works just as well. If you do use yellow glue, use track nails to hold the roadbed in place as the glue dries.

First, separate the cork roadbed into two strips (fig. 1-27). Each strip has a beveled and a straight edge. The straight edges butt

Continued on page 22

Fig. 1-32. To avoid inhaling paint fumes, Ric is spray-painting the base color and multitextured paint outside.

Fig. 1-33. A rainbow sets behind Maude Frickett's house situated in the Indian Bluffs as an ATSF 4-6-2 Pacific steam engine approaches with the evening passenger train. After it's been painted and scenicked, the multi-textured paint produces very realistic rockwork.

Fig. 1-35. This action photograph clearly demonstrates dual-cab wiring. Insulated rail joiners between the engines separate the track into two electrical blocks controlled with the same power pack. The power to the left block is on, making the locomotive move, and the right block is off, bringing that engine to a standstill.

One- and Two-Train Wiring

One-train wiring (also known as one-cab control) is the simplest to wire. You already have everything you need to operate your layout this way. With the power pack turned off, use 22 gauge wire to connect the DC terminals to a terminal track (fig. 1-34). Once you have assembled and connected all the track, plug in the power pack, turn the power on, give your engine some power by rotating the speed knob, and you're in business.

What could possibly be more fun than running one train? A second train running around the Great N-pire Railroad, of course! Each train has its own separate engineer, so they can do their work independently (fig. 1-35). In the business of scale model railroading this is known as dual-cab control. Although it sounds complicated, taken slowly it really is quite simple to wire. Dual-cab control has several advantages: you can run one train all the time, run two trains (one at a time) from one power pack

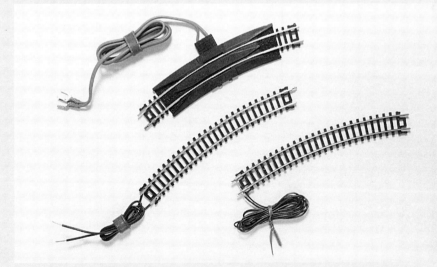

Fig. 1-34. Here are three common ways of attaching feeder wires (terminal leads) from the power pack to the track. The top section is a manufacturer's terminal track, the middle section has the feeder wires soldered directly to the track, and the lower section uses rail joiners with presoldered wires.

Fig. 1-36. A close-up photograph shows the insulating rail joiners separating the track into two blocks, with the electrifying rail joiners and feeder wires to the right.

through block control, or run two trains independently from two power packs. The Great N-pire Railroad will live up to its full operational potential if wired for dual-cab control. Complete dual-cab control requires four things: the layout insulated into electrical blocks, a second locomotive, a second power pack available for the second train (if you upgraded your first pack, you now have two), and an electrical control panel to transfer the control of the track blocks back and forth between power packs.

Isolate the layout into electrical blocks by using insulated rail joiners (fig. 1-36). Insulated rail joiners prevent electricity from flowing automatically from one section of track to another. Only when you route the power from the power pack through a control panel's electric switch to a specific track block does that portion of the track become electrified, allowing the locomotive to move.

Figure 1-37 shows four different insulated blocks of the east-west main line and switching yard. As an example, using fig. 1-37, a mainline freight would stop and wait in block 2 while a switcher pulls a string of box cars out of block 4 into block 3. After the track switch is thrown the switcher proceeds into block 1. Once the switcher is clear of block 3 the freight can proceed ahead into block 3, vacating block 2 for the switcher train. This is how the real railroads operate! If you were not going to expand the railroad, you'll probably want to section the east-west mainline oval into four blocks instead of three, so that each of the two trains would always have one clear block ahead to move into. (See fig. 1-38 for an optional insulated blocking pattern.) This way you'll have six different electrical blocks at

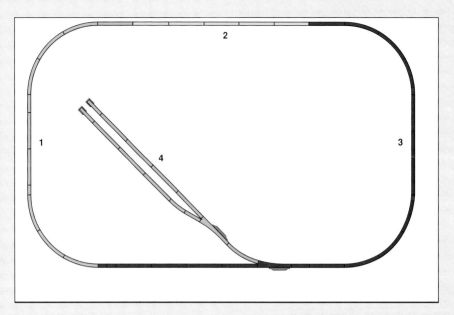

Fig. 1-37. This is the mainline and industrial switching yard, separated into four electrical blocks. Only three electrical blocks are used instead of four on the main line because of track placement through all of the expansions.

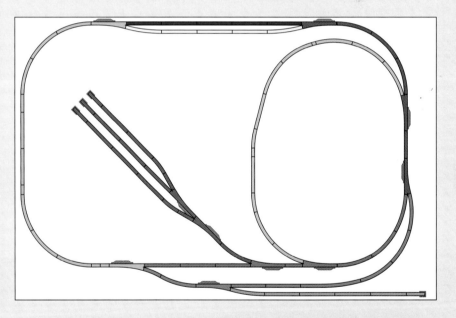

Fig. 1-38. This is an optional blocking pattern if you plan to build the layout only through phase 2. You need four mainline blocks for two trains unless you incorporate the additional ovals and passing tracks in the later expansions.

the end of phase 2 development.

When you wire the control panel, it will be much easier if you understand how power routes through double-pole, double-throw (DPDT) electrical switches (fig. 1-39). One-cab wiring connected the feeder wires from the power pack to the track without any electrical switches in between. Dual-cab wiring connects the feeder wires from the power pack through the DPDT block switches to the track. The right power pack feeder wires connect to the left switch posts, the left power pack feeder wire connect to the right switch posts, and the

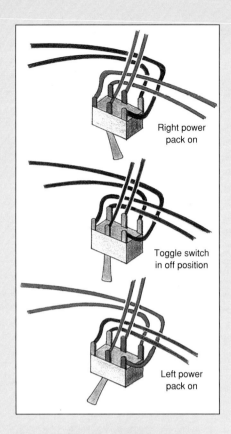

Fig. 1-40. Corner molding protects the fragile foam-core edge. Notice the difference between the spray paint on the tabletop and the sides, representing two colors.

Fig. 1-39. This trio of DPDT switches illustrates the flow of current in relation to the toggle switch position. In the top diagram the toggle, by being thrown to the right, connects the right power pack through the red wires to the track. The middle diagram displays the off position in black. In the bottom diagram the toggle connects the left power pack to the track through the red wires.

track feeder wires connect to the center posts. If you connect the power packs to opposite switch posts, the toggle switch becomes an indicator of which power pack is in use. The toggle switch points to the right when the right power pack is on and to the left when the left power pack is on. This is all the circuitry you need to know to operate your layout. You will do the control panel wiring after you lay track.

together in the middle, and the beveled edges create the ballast slope. Now lay down an 8" to 12" line of hot glue along the inside curve of the track pattern. Align the inner edge of the roadbed with the center of track pattern while pressing and bending the roadbed to the curve. Hold it in position until the glue sets (fig. 1-28).

After gluing one half of the roadbed, lay down a line of glue following the other side of the track pattern (fig. 1-29). Press, curve, and hold the other half of the roadbed in place until the glue hardens. Continue around the track pattern in this manner up to the industrial yard switch. The switch requires a special roadbed pattern. The ends of the roadbed strip become misaligned as you progress. You'll trim the ends flush when you complete the oval.

Roadbed under switches (fig. 1-30) supports the track and either the switch machine or the ground throw. Create the roadbed support under the switch

machine by turning a length of roadbed so the beveled edges match. Complete the roadbed oval by doing an overlap cut on the ends. Now you can complete the industrial yard spurs with roadbed and finish the process by cutting off the overlapping ends (fig. 1-31).

Painting the Scenery Base

Remember our discussion of the three basic scenery elements—shape, color, and texture? Your trainboard has started to take on shape, and now its earth needs a color to transform it into a landscape. Many model railroaders use a good-quality brand of house paint to add texture. A flat water-soluble latex in a base tint or tan works very well. You will add actual dirt for soil, and a textured ground cover mix (grass) over the paint, but if the base coat is too dark your miniature world won't look correct. Use a roller and tray to paint the flat tabletop and a wide brush on the rougher bluffs. The roadbed gets painted as well—after all, it is really a berm of formed earth. A faster interesting method is to use a multicolored textured spray paint. Textured paint is more expensive than house paint but the results are well worth the cost. House paint is designed for flat, even color, while textured spray paint is a mix of three different colors with an uneven texture.

As always, don your safety equipment, then head outdoors or to a well-ventilated garage to start painting (fig. 1-32). We recommend spraying the trainboard first with a spray paint similar in color to the textured spray paint. A pre-spray covers the white base and reduces the amount of the textured spray paint you'll need. We used a Krylon spray paint, no. 2412 light peach, as an undercoat and Plasti-kote Fleckstone, no. 438 canyon rock as the ground color (fig. 1-33). After painting the entire trainboard tabletop with either type of paint, paint the sides a contrasting color. We chose a slate blue paint as a complementary hue. You can use spray paint to cover the sides quickly, but be sure to mask and protect the painted top.

The next step is to trim the trainboard with corner and edge molding (fig. 1-40). The difficult work of mitering 45-degree angles at the molding's corners is simplified by using a miter box and saw combination. After you cut the corners, stain the molding to accent the wood grain. Then attach the molding to the foam core with yellow glue and track nails every 6".

You may need to clamp the flat molding along the bottom edge until the glue dries. Sections of masking tape strapped over the molding and up the sides every few inches will also hold it in

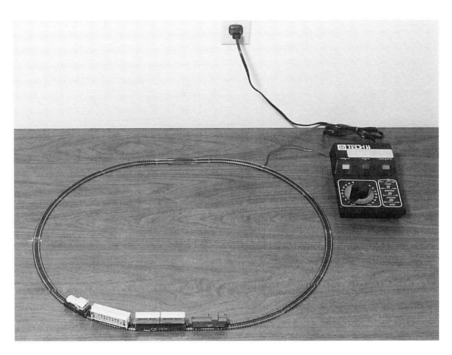

Fig. 1-41. A single transformer (power pack) powers the entire oval through a single pair of feeder wires, making the oval one electrical block. This common form of wiring is known as one-cab control.

place. After the paint has dried and the molding is in place, stand back and admire your handiwork. Now you're about to make tracks and cover a lot of ground.

Electrical Wiring Principles, Power Packs, and Couplers

Model railroad locomotives are powered by miniature electric motors that operate on modified electrical current provided by a standard household outlet (fig. 1-41). Wiring can sometimes be

intimidating, but it is really fairly simple to wire the Great N-pire Railroad if you know the principles and follow our step-by-step instruction.

Power packs are the mysterious black boxes that run the locomotives. Think of them as stationary tenders that hold the fuel ready for your engines to use. Figure 1-42 explains what a power pack does—how it changes the household electrical current into "locomotive fuel." Inside a power pack you'll find a transformer that

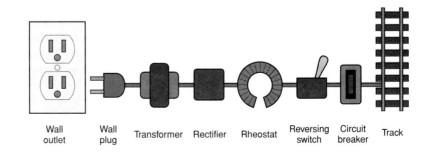

Wall outlet   Wall plug   Transformer   Rectifier   Rheostat   Reversing switch   Circuit breaker   Track

Fig. 1-42. This is a diagrammatic view of what is inside the "black box" of a power pack. The raw electrical current from the wall outlet is reduced, transformed, controlled, and protected by the power pack.

Fig. 1-43. The difference between Rapido horn-style couplers (installed on the left-hand boxcar) and Kadee realistic knuckle couplers (installed on the right-hand boxcar) is apparent.

Fig. 1-44. Model Power makes this plunger-style electric uncoupling ramp to uncouple Rapido horn-type couplers automatically.

Fig. 1-45. We installed a shortened Kadee magnetic uncoupling ramp on our pike in the short straight track section just before the track switch to the industrial yard.

reduces the high-voltage household alternating current (AC) to a lesser voltage appropriate for model locomotives' miniature motors. Although the voltage is lower, alternating current is the wrong "fuel" for your engines. A rectifier then uses diodes to change the AC, which flows in two directions, into single direction direct current (DC). Next, a rheostat is the control in a power pack that you use most. This is the engine cab throttle that varies the speed of your locomotives. Real engines also have a reversing gear to change direction; a power pack utilizes an electric switch to reverse the electric current's polarity, which changes the direction of the engine. Finally, a circuit breaker prevents your locomotives from receiving too much current, which would burn out a motor.

Power packs that come with train sets work fine, but they are often inadequate for a railroad's needs. As soon as you can afford it, you'll want to upgrade your power pack to a more powerful one. Your local hobby dealer can help you make the appropriate selection based on your requirements. Don't throw that old one away! You can use it for powering additional accessories, such as lights, later on.

Uncoupling with Kadee or Rapido Couplers. Coupling, uncoupling, spotting cars, picking them up, and moving them to another location is a significant part of the operation of the model railroad. N scale trains rely on two different types of couplers, Kadee or Rapido, to keep the train together (fig. 1-43). Most manufacturers of engines and cars come equipped with the Rapido type of coupler making the equipment ready to run as is. You have to purchase and install

Fig. 1-46a. This is the normal closed position of a Kadee coupler between cars. This position connects the cars together into a train.

Fig. 1-46b. This is the open or uncoupled position of a Kadee coupler when it is stopped over a Kadee magnetic uncoupling ramp.

Kadee couplers separately. There are advantages as well as disadvantages to both kinds.

Although their appearance does not resemble real knuckle couplers, the simple design of Rapido couplers makes them very reliable. These couplers pivot in their sockets and couple by riding up and over one another. In order to uncouple a car, you must manually lift one coupler up and over the other. This often results in having to rerail the car afterward. An electric plunger-style uncoupling ramp is available for Rapido couplers (fig. 1-44), but like the couplers themselves it is unrealistic. You can build a simple uncoupling tool to facilitate uncoupling by hand by bending a piece of wire into an L. This "hands on" uncoupling is similar to the way the real railroads do it with uncoupler lift bars.

Kadee couplers resemble prototype knuckle couplers and operate by magnetism. A magnetized uncoupling ramp (fig. 1-45) causes the couplers to swing apart when they pass over it (figs. 1-46a and 1-46b) The engineer first spots the end of the car he wants uncoupled by stopping it over the ramp (figs. 1-46a and

1-46b). Then he slowly backs up, which separates the couplers. As the engine pulls forward, the car or string of cars is left behind. Reversing the engine again, the engineer can push the car backwards into position wherever it's supposed to be on the track. Watch a real switching yard sometime and you'll see the same actions! Of all the equipment available to the model railroad enthusiast none comes more highly recommended than Kadee couplers. Realistic-looking Kadee couplers facilitate a layout's operation by minimizing handling. For these reasons most serious N scale modelers eventually convert all of their rolling stock and equipment to Kadee couplers.

If you choose to use Kadee couplers, it's smart to convert your railroad cars as you acquire them. Converting rolling stock is generally easy. All you have to do is replace the truck and wheelset with the Micro Train version, which comes with preinstalled Kadee couplers. Micro Train cars come pre-equipped with Kadee couplers and are well worth the price—they are prototypically accurate and exquisitely detailed. Kadee also sells many

coupler conversion kits for diesels and steam locomotives with complete instructions.

Laying Track

It's time to whistle up that work train and roust out all those would-be John Henrys—there's track waiting to be laid. Be sure that the work train has the track listed in Table 1-5. You already know the sequence of track pieces, because you laid out the track plan once before. The only changes now are the insulated joiners for block control (fig. 1-37)

Table 1-5. Tracklaying Supplies

- Painted track pieces
- Insulated rail joiners
- Terminal rail joiners with presoldered feeder wires
- 2 no. 206S Caboose Industries ground throws
- Kadee magnetic uncoupling ramp
- Track-cleaning block
- Wire track nails and nailset
- X-acto knife
- Scribe or sharp awl
- Power pack and engine

Fig. 1-47. Ric checks the trackwork by sighting down a laid section.

Fig. 1-48. We discovered that the grade transition from the baseboard of the tabletop to the Indian Bluffs was not level—it had a dip. We leveled the grade by inserting a thin block of sheet styrene over the dip in the roadbed and under the track. Later, we'll cover it with ballast.

and terminal rail joiners with feeder wires, which electrify the track. Review fig. 1-10 for the correct placement of the insulated rail joiners. The electrical blocks have specific locations on the track plan.

The importance of careful trackwork cannot be stressed enough. The better the trackwork, the smoother your trains will run. Track pieces held together by rail joiners should have no height discrepancies, kinks, gaps, or sharp edges. These can cause locomotive and car derailments. Correct any of these faults by realignment, replacing the pieces in question, or carefully filing and rounding the rail edges. All straight lengths should be straight and true as well as level from side to side. Check your straights by sighting down the middle of the track at track level (fig. 1-47). Curves and the grade transitions between track elevations should be smooth and continuous. We had a dip on both of the ramps leading to the Indian Bluffs. We corrected it by inserting a piece of styrene between the track and the roadbed (fig. 1-48). The styrene wedge will be hidden under the ballast. Such corrections now will save you

headaches later on when you want to concentrate on operating your trains.

Figure 1-49 illustrates how to secure track on the roadbed. Each piece of track has a predrilled nail hole through two or more ties. Gently push a track nail with a standard nail set through the tie hole into the roadbed and foam core until the nailhead is flush with the top of the tie. Be careful, as too much pressure will bend or crack a plastic tie and distort the rails. Too little pressure, however, will not hold the track in place. Track nails also make it easy to remove those track sections that you change and replace during future expansions. The glue and ballast mixture will permanently bond track to the roadbed—so leave the ballasting until after all the trackwork is finished. Each insulated track block must have its own set of feeder wires leading from the track to the control panel and power pack. Make it easy on yourself by using terminal rail joiners presoldered with wire leads. Remember to clean the paint from the rail sides before soldering, or the soldered connection will be insulated and current will not flow through it.

Begin laying track at the same place as you started your track plan. Notice that the insulated rail joiners are between the first and second straight sections and the sixth and seventh straight sections. Place the terminal rail joiners between the second and third sections. Check the track for straight alignment and then clean the paint from only the top of the rails with an abrasive cleaning block. Do not use sandpaper to clean the paint off. Once the rail tops are shiny clean, hook up the terminal feed wires to the power pack and test an engine back and forth across the straight section. Always test each insulated block before laying the next one. Any electrical continuity problems are easier to find and fix before all the track is laid.

Once you are satisfied with your first track block, start laying the second track block. Stop at the 4½" section to install the Kadee uncoupling magnet You'll have to shorten the uncoupling magnet—it is too long for this section of track. Measure the distance between the molded ends of the short track section. Mark the magnet the same length by removing equal amounts from

Fig. 1-49. Set the track in place, using track nails and a nailset to push them in. Apply enough pressure to set them firmly but not enough pressure to bend or break the plastic ties.

both ends. Scribe a line across the magnet and use a pair of pliers to snap the short end off along the scribed line. Next cut the ties out between the rails with an X-acto knife, leaving the molded spikes to hold the rails in gauge. Carefully align the magnet inside the cut ties and glue it in place. Be sure that the magnet is not higher than the rail height and that the gap between the magnet and the rails is equal and parallel. Use the terminal rail joiners and feeder wires to connect

the uncoupling magnet section to the existing track.

Finish laying the track to the insulated rail joiners before the third curve, then test it as you did before. Follow the same procedure to complete the oval and industrial switching yard. Now you'll install the ground throws (fig. 1-50), unless you decided to have an Atlas manual or electric switch machine. Now that the track is fastened to the roadbed and it has passed inspection and electrical continuity tests, you're ready to construct the track block control panel.

Wiring the Block Control Panel

The time has finally come to add power to the rails of the Great N-pire Railroad. Assemble the materials from Table 1-6 and make a photocopy of fig. 1-51, a drawing of the layout template that will become the control panel. The circles will be cut out for mounting the electric DPDT switches that control the electrical track blocks.

Fig. 1-50. An exploded diagrammatic view of installing Caboose Industries' ground throws.

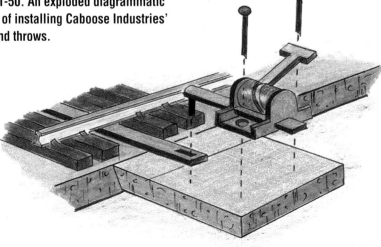

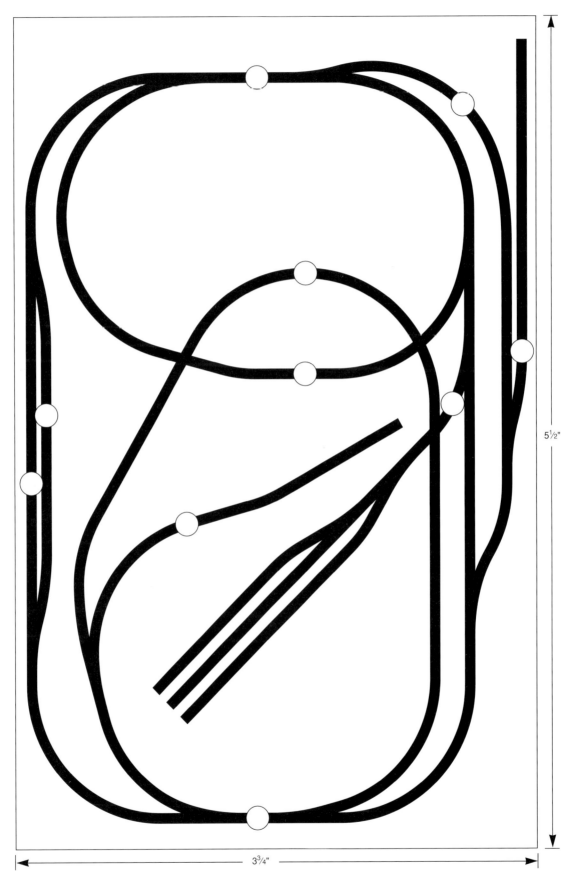

5½"

3¾"

Fig. 1-51. Reduce this track plan diagram by 35 percent on a photocopy machine and glue it to a 3¾" x 5½" piece of matte board. Cut out the holes for the DPDT electrical switches and mount, following the instructions for the track block control panel.

Table 1-6. Control Panel and Wiring Supplies

- CAD template for control panel (photocopy fig. 1-51)
- 4 DPDT Micro electric switches for block wiring
- 2 two-conductor ¼" phone plugs, jacks, and sockets
- 2 ⅜" flat washers
- no. 22 gauge wire and wire nippers
- Sheet styrene
- Wire nuts
- Hand-held soldering gun and resin-core solder
- X-acto knife and small awl
- ¼" hole punch
- Hot glue gun and glue, yellow glue
- Masking tape
- Power pack

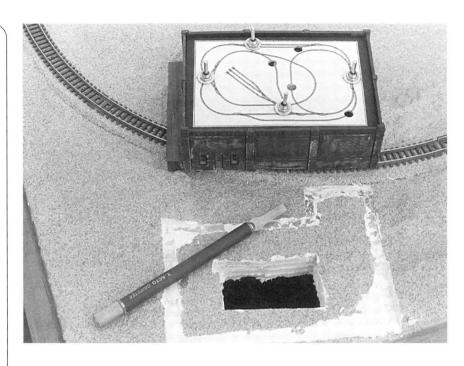

Fig. 1-52. This is the rectangular hole for the control panel that we cut in the baseboard in the southwest corner of the layout.

Locate the control panel in the southwest corner of the layout. You can mount it directly onto the trainboard or use it as a roof to the Electrical Switch and Industrial Siding Co. building. You don't have to build the building right now. We will, however, illustrate the installation of the control panel with the completed and assembled building.

Glue the photocopy of the track plan template onto a sheet of styrene, artboard, or matte board. If you are mounting it directly to the trainboard, make the board or sheet 3¾" x 5½". If you are using it as a roof, make it 3⁷⁄₁₆" x 5⅛". Cut out the circles with an X-acto knife or the hole punch and mount the DPDT switches so the levers throw right and left.

Trace the control board rectangle on the southwest corner and level the area with an X-acto knife. Cut a rectangular hole approximately 1½" x 3" through the tabletop for the wiring to pass through (fig. 1-52).

If you are using the control panel by itself, without the building, here's how to proceed: After drilling holes into the trainboard, fasten it to the trainboard with a long bolt, washer, and nut combination in each corner. Punch a hole with the awl through the trainboard near each terminal rail

joiner and thread the feeder wires through the hole to the underside (fig. 1-53). Measure the distance from each hole to the control panel and cut two lengths of wire 1 foot longer for each set. Trim the insulation from the ends of the wire length, twist together with the appropriate terminal

Fig. 1-53. The ease of foam core: use an awl to punch a hole through the trainboard base so you can run the track feeder wires through to the control panel.

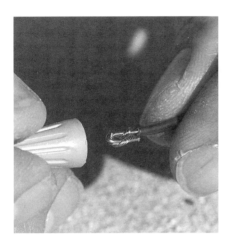

Fig. 1-54. Connect (splice) the wire ends together by using a wire nut. Then you don't have to solder them.

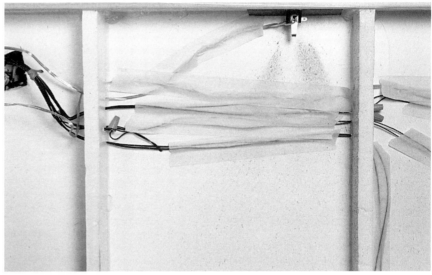

Fig. 1-55. On the underside of the trainboard make holes for the wiring through the necessary stringers and joists using an awl as before. After the wiring is complete masking tape secures the wiring to the underside, keeping it out of the way.

feeder wire, and secure with a wire nut (fig. 1-54). Mark each pair of wires for the outside and inside rail and which block they belong to. If the inside and outside rails are switched, you will create an electrical short when you turn the power on. String the wires across the trainboard's underside to the control panel opening. Use the awl to create holes in the stringers and braces for the wires. Masking tape secures the wires to the underside (fig. 1-55).

Fig. 1-56. A ¼" phone jack outlet hole covered by a ⅜" washer is visible on the trainboard side to the right of the Electrical Switch and Industrial Siding Co. building, which houses the control panel.

At this point we added an additional feature to our wiring plan. We installed a standard ¼" phone jack and plug between the control panel and the power pack to provide a solid, yet portable, power connection. Begin by fastening the jacks on small rectangles of thick cardboard using a nut and bolt assembly. Next cut out two ⅜" holes on the trainboard's south side and hot-glue

the two washers around the openings to protect the foam core (fig. 1-56). Run two lengths (with the extra foot) of wire from the jacks to the control panel.

Now it's time to heat up your soldering gun and "hard-wire" the control panel. Start by threading the wires through the eyes on the electrical switch posts, following the diagram in fig. 1-57 and twisting them together. Connect all the outside rail lines to the same post on each of the electrical switches. The purpose of soldering is to ensure the electrical connection, not to hold the wires in place. Soldering is easy, but if you fail to use the proper technique, you can make what is known as "cold" joints, which inhibit the electrical current or do not allow it flow at all. Start by "tinning" the tip of the soldering iron with a little solder. Use only resin-core solder, not acid-core solder. Now place the tip on one side of the connection to be soldered to heat it up. Touch the connection with the solder in the other hand, allowing it to melt and flow into the joint. This creates an excellent electrical connection, a "hot" joint.

Connect and solder the wires from the left-hand phone jack as shown in the wiring diagram. Cut additional pieces of wire, then trim, connect, and solder all the electrical switch posts in the pattern illustrated. Follow this procedure for the right-hand cab control, too. Now connect and solder wire to the phone jacks. Do the same to the phone plug and connect the terminal ends, but do not solder them to the power pack. Finally, bundle all the wires together with a wire tie. Then fasten the control panel onto the trainboard or press it into place as the building roof.

Now it's time to run the trains. Plug the power pack into the wall outlet. Be sure the pack is in the off position. Push the phone plug into the left-hand phone jack and throw all the switches on the control panel to the left position. Put your engine on the track, turn the power pack on,

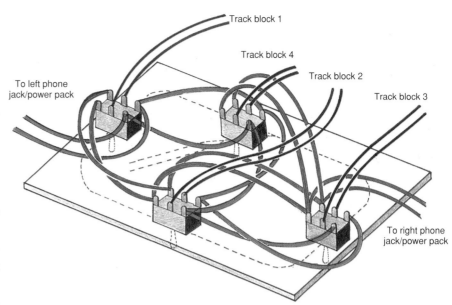

Fig. 1-57. This is the master wiring diagram on the underside of the control panel from the photocopy of fig. 1-51. All black wires go from the center posts to the track—be sure that each side is connected to the same rail. All blue wiring goes to the phone jack outlet on the right-hand power pack, and all red wiring goes to the phone jack outlet on the left-hand power pack.

and throttle up slowly. Congratulations, Casey—you're finally an engineer!

If you aren't quite highballing around the pike, check your engine first. Next, try throwing all the control panel electrical switches to the right, then check for power; see if all the other proper electrical switches are thrown properly. If still nothing happens, apply the troubleshooting steps on another section of the layout. If all else fails, you'll

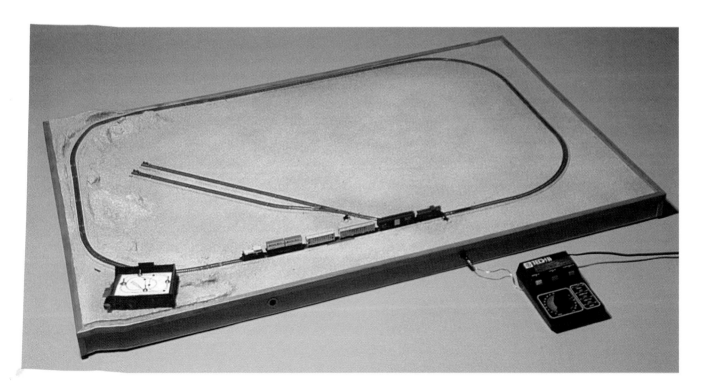

Fig. 1-58. At the end of this section your layout should look something like this, with operating trains!

Fig. 1-59. Ric collects neighborhood dirt with a trowel. Before using it as soil, remove most of the large particles by sifting.

Fig. 1-60. The refining process starts at left with raw collected dirt. Sift it first through an ordinary kitchen strainer and then through a tea strainer.

have to check every connection from the power pack to the rails. If your power pack's forward and reverse switches do not match the locomotive's direction of travel, try reversing the wire leads of the phone jack that are attached to the back of the power pack. Don't forget to test the right-hand cab control as well.

Most likely, though, your locomotive is winding its way around the track bringing the Great N-pire Railroad to life (fig. 1-58). Create a train and try uncoupling and switching. All you have left to do is build a building or two and landscape with ground cover.

Basic Ground Cover

The ground and bluffs you sculpted have a nice form but look rather desolate. Multiple layers of soil, grass, and bushes over the textured paint can easily provide a look of vegetated ground cover. Try collecting your own dirt for soil as we did, and use Woodland Scenics turf for grass and ground foam for bushes. A single soil-and-grass combination

Fig. 1-61. This is a collection of different-color soil mixtures at the bottom, with shrubbery (ground foam) in the middle and turf (grass) on top. Use them in combination to give different colors to different areas on the layout.

Table 1-7. Ground Cover Supplies

- Matte medium diluted with water 1:6
- Soil mixtures—red, tan, and brown
- Turfs—earth, green grass, weeds
- Bushes (coarse turf)—burnt, light green, dark green
- Wide paintbrush
- Sifters—1 coarse kitchen strainer, 1 tea strainer
- Eyedroppers
- Spray bottle with a fine mist

would work for the entire layout, but three different color combinations help achieve a realistic effect. Red soil and dry buff-colored grass are appropriate for Indian Bluffs, tan soil and light green grass will separate the valley from the bluffs and give it contrast, while the east end will appear more fertile with a darker, richer soil and lush green grass.

Collecting different colors of dirt is not difficult—we found several colors within our neighborhood (fig. 1-59). Next we sifted each twice through two different strainers to produce a finer, more usable grade. The first sifter is a standard household strainer, and the second is a tea strainer, which has a finer mesh. The first sifting separates the boulders from the rough soil; the second sifting produces a fine grade of soil and takes out the rocks (fig. 1-60). If you can't find soil in three different colors, you can mix in prepackaged ground cover. Be sure to write down the combinations and proportions in case you run out.

Use a mixture of dilute glue and water to bind the soil and turf to the trainboard. You can

Fig. 1-63. A collection of soil sifters (besides your own fingers) that are easy to find. No, that is not cinnamon or Italian seasoning—it is scale soil and shrubbery.

use white glue and water, but this doesn't work as well as artist's matte medium, an acrylic polymer used in painting, available at your local art supply store. Mix a solution of one part glue or matte medium to six parts water and store it in a glass jar.

Assemble the supplies and tools in Table 1-7 (fig. 1-61), and you'll become a landscaper. Start on Indian Bluffs by painting a thin layer of the diluted matte medium or glue mixture over the

top surfaces (fig. 1-62). First practice sifting soil by shaking and tapping it over plain paper to get a feel for the process. Shakers, sifters, and fingers work equally well (fig. 1-63). Cover the ground with the soil lightly and intermittently, allowing some textured base color to show through. When you near the edge of the glue-painted area, reduce the amount of soil so you can blend it into the

Continued on page 39

Fig. 1-62. Start applying the ground cover by painting diluted **matte** medium over the area to be covered.

Fig. 1-64. Here Ric uses his fingers to dust the ground cover. Fingers are as adept as any mechanical sifter.

Fig. 1-65. This is a comparison between an unpainted Life-Like rural station on the left and the painted version in our railroad's color scheme on the right.

The Enville Train Station

The train station is the first structure most railroads build for their passenger service. We chose Life-Like's rural passenger station (no. 7431) as our first plastic building kit on the Great N-pire Railroad. This building has the architecture of a small American train station, complete with bay windows. The finished station will fit perfectly alongside the oval east end.

You could assemble the rural passenger station without any modifications, but it would only look like a model. Careful painting and weathering will turn it into a miniature version of the real building. We'll show you two ways you can finish the structure (fig. 1-65). But how

Fig. 1-66. Dull the "plastic" sheen of a building kit by using ordinary household cleanser and a toothbrush. This step is not necessary if you plan to paint your structure.

Fig. 1-67. You can also use Testor's Dullcote to deaden the sheen of plastic models or glossy paints.

Fig. 1-68. Spray-paint the larger areas of the building's walls for an even, finished coat but paint all the detail castings on the buildings by hand using small brushes.

you finish the kit is up to you. **Dulling the plastic.** Temporarily exchange your engineer's cap for a hard hat and order the construction supplies in Table 1-8. For both versions, leave all the parts attached to the sprue until the final assembly stage. Plastic kits are wonderful for modelers, but the material certainly does not look real. If you like the molded colors of the station, use the following trick to speed up construction. Dull the plastic sheen with household cleanser and a toothbrush as shown in fig. 1-66. Gently scrub the entire surface and rinse it with running water when the surface dulls. After this technique,

Enville Station is ready for a weathering treatment.

Painting. Model paints come in two varieties: water-based and solvent-based. Today modelers are fortunate to have a wide variety of water-based paints. Unless you are spray-painting from a can we recommend using a water-based paint. Some companies even manufacture specific railroad colors. The major differences between paints are their flow characteristics and drying time. Each paint is a bit different, but all of them produce excellent results.

Most things in nature have a flat finish. Our preference is to use flat paints unless they are unavailable. Gloss paints can be

made flat by an overspray of Testor's Dullcote, a matte lacquer overcoat spray (fig. 1-67). However, we'll apply our recommended weathering treatment of alcohol and ink before using Dullcote. Glossy objects such as glass windows, water, and clean locomotives will naturally stand out from the flat matte finish surroundings. A gloss finish applied to anything will make that item a focal point. Use the difference between gloss and flat finishes to draw attention to a special locomotive or a window that has interior detail.

Railroads often have a standard color scheme for their buildings. Painting each of them the same

Fig. 1-69. Apply the weathering alcohol wash in downward strokes with a very large flat brush and allow it to air dry.

Fig. 1-70. The roof section demonstrates the radical improvement weathering gives the model by accenting the cracks and leaving irregular deposits on the model's surfaces.

Fig. 1-71. The final weathering step is a technique called drybrushing. Remove most of the paint from the brush, and brush what remains lightly downward across the surface, giving highlights to raised portions of the casting. In combination with the base color and the alcohol wash, drybrushing produces realism.

Fig. 1-72. Resist any temptation to twist model pieces from the casting sprue. Always nip them or cut them with a hobby knife. Paint as much as possible while the pieces are still attached to the sprue. You can touch up the small unpainted areas later.

Fig. 1-73. After removing the pieces from the sprue, file the edge smooth with a flat file or emery board. Touch up the painting, if necessary.

way unifies the buildings and presents them as property of the railroad company. We decided to paint the second version of our station in a classic railroad color combination. We selected golden yellow for the sides, dark green for the overall wood trim, white for the window trim, and red for the roof. All other railroad structures will be painted the same colors. Paint every part while it is still attached to the sprue, then touch up the structure after assembly. We spray-painted the sides and roof for an even finish. Spray-painting leaves only the windows and trim to be painted by brush (fig. 1-68). Brush-painting will also work for all these purposes.

Weathering is an important technique for aging a model that adds to the effect of realism. It is important not to overdo weathering—a little weathering goes a long way. The method of weathering we use takes two steps: the first stage uses a dark wash, which adds depth while darkening the cracks and seams; the second stage uses a brushing of light color that represents fading and enhances the details. We found two different colored alcohol washes that work well. Mix one tablespoon of india ink with one pint of isopropyl alcohol (rubbing alcohol), available at your drug or food store. The other wash is mixed in the same proportion, substituting brown ink for the black. The black wash is used for cold colors like gray and blue. The brown wash works on white and warm colors like yellow and represents rust stains.

Alcohol will damage your fine paintbrushes, so choose a wide, cheap brush to use only for these washes. Shake the wash to suspend the ink particles, dip in your brush, and stroke downward over the surfaces, not from side to side (fig. 1-69). As the alcohol evaporates the ink particles will be deposited along edges and in scribed lines. This process adds shadows to the model and dirties the surface (fig. 1-70).

Our final weathering step involves drybrushing with one or two highlight colors. In drybrushing you remove most of the paint from the brush and then streak it lightly downward over the model area (fig. 1-71). The first highlight color is a lighter or different shade of the color you painted the model. You can mix a lighter value by adding white to your chosen color. The second highlight color is white. After these finishes your building will look as if it has been in place for years.

Preparation and glues. Resist the temptation to twist the plastic parts from the sprue—it will ruin the parts' edges. Always cut the part from the sprue with an X-acto knife, a pair of nippers, or side cutters (fig. 1-72). File any remaining plastic with a large flat file or even an ordinary emery board (fig. 1-73). Check all parts against one another for a proper fit, and correct any burr or flashing with a knife, file, or sandpaper. Be careful not to leave fingerprints on the freshly painted surfaces.

Any liquid cement will work for gluing your plastic buildings together. Apply liquid cements with a fine artist's brush. We prefer Pacer Technology's Zap Gap, a "super" glue, for cementing the parts together. Zap Gap uses a fine-tip applicator called a Z-End, which reduces and controls the glue flow. A tip is essential for applying the glue where you need it. *Follow all instructions when using glues. Super glue can be dangerous. Do not get it on your skin or between your fingers,*

Fig. 1-74. Cut windows from clear styrene or acetate with a scissors. Cut them a little larger than the openings and glue them in place at the overlapped corners. Apply glue sparingly, or capillary action will make the glue appear in the windows.

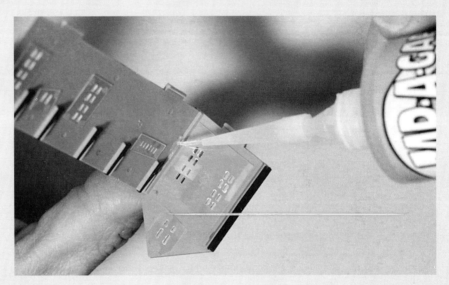

Fig. 1-75. We use Zap Gap, a "super glue," for almost everything. Other glues work equally well. Your hobby shop salesman will be happy to advise you.

and especially keep it away from your eyes. Pacer makes a debonder, but more than one modeler has ended up in the emergency room for minor surgery.

Windows are an important architectural feature of any building. Often the "glass" included in model building kits is unrealistically thick. Some modelers even use real microscope slide cover glass for their windows. We won't go to that extreme—we'll just use a clear styrene available

from Evergreen Products. Handle clear styrene by the edges or with the tissue provided because it acquires scratches and fingerprints easily. Use scissors to cut each window pattern a little larger than the window opening, then glue in place (fig. 1-74). Be careful—too much glue can flow across the styrene and mar the viewable portion. You can also simulate broken or open windows by using X-acto knives and scissors to trim them out.

Fig. 1-76. It is important to seal the edges between the building and the ground to give the building the look of having been built from the ground up. After laying down a small bead of matte medium, tap in more asphalt with a teaspoon.

Fig. 1-77. Tamp the asphalt in place with a tongue depressor or popsicle stick, thus hiding the crack between the building and the ground.

Fig. 1-78. Santa Fe's morning passenger train pulls up to a nicely detailed station to pick up passengers for the morning commuter run. The exquisite wig-wag is courtesy of Sunrise Enterprises.

Final assembly. The most challenging part of building any structure is keeping the sides square to one another. Since the rural station kit was made for glueless snap assembly, square corners are built in. Press the front wall with the bay window into the base as shown in the directions. Add an end wall and glue along the inside edge where the glue can't be seen (fig. 1-75). Continue the assembly with the second end wall and then the back. Insert the eave supports and then glue them and the chimney into place. *Do not glue the roof.* You'll want to remove the roof later when you insert miniature interior lights.

Installation and details. The Enville Station is complete but not finished. Two short straight track sections on the mainline oval's east end mark the location of the train station. The two standard straight sections on both sides of the short sections will be replaced by track switches during expansion of the Great N-pire. We were about to install our station when an idea occurred to us. Since we had an extra Atlas rerailer ramp track section, we thought it would look better than the ordinary short pieces. Not only would the ramp mark the train track as the station stop, it would also provide a pedestrian crossing ramp between the station and the town site. We cut off both ends to the proper length, filed the rail ends square, painted it, and installed it.

Scrape away the vegetation over the area where the station will go to create an asphalt parking lot and base for the structure. Arizona Rock and Mineral Co. sells a premade mixture of asphalt similar to the soil we used as the first layer of ground cover. A dark gray flat latex house paint would work almost as well and act as glue at the same time. Prepare the area as you did for ground cover, first painting dilute matte medium and then sifting the asphalt mixture over it.

The next step is to glue the station to the tabletop. Any number of strong adhesives or glues would work including yellow glue, full strength matte medium, or Weldbond. Lay a bead of glue along the bottom edge of the sides of the station and then press it in place next to the track. The wooden platform aligned with the edge of the roadbed not only squares the building to the track but also provides proper clearance between the structure and the track.

Building foundations are details often overlooked on a layout. In real life buildings have some type of foundation sunk into the ground or a basement. Many modelers do not fill in this gap between the building and the tabletop and thereby destroy any realistic effect. Always fill this gap with the same ground cover that surrounds the building. Use a small brush to paint a bead of dilute matte medium along the bottom edge of the structure. A teaspoon is a useful tool for sprinkling the ground cover over the bead of matte medium (fig. 1-76). Finally, use a tongue depressor or popsicle stick to press the ground cover flat (fig. 1-77).

Added details will enhance your structures, making them look lived-in and used. It is always easier to add details as you go rather than waiting until every structure is built—besides there are always more details to add. Model Power makes a number of accessory sets. Other manufactures make details such as people. In the next stage we'll discuss painting and detailing human figures.

Fig. 1-79. Dribble matte medium over the rocks, using an eyedropper or brush. It will glue them to the surface, creating talus slopes, boulder areas, and rubble at the bottom of slopes.

Table 1-9. E.S.&I.S. Co. Supplies

Design Preservation Models
- 1 street/dock level blank wall
- 1 street/dock level entry doors
- 1 dock level freight doors
- 2 dock riser walls

Evergreen styrene
- 1 strip styrene .080" x .080" no. 269-164
- 1 sheet styrene V-Groove .025"
- 1 sheet clear styrene .010"

- Layout template with holes cut and mounted on a 3$\frac{7}{16}$" x 5$\frac{1}{8}$" board or styrene
- X-acto knife and blades
- Flat file or emery board
- Zap Gap glue or equivalent

next section. Next, sprinkle on the turf for grass. The grass should be patchy, just as it is in real life (fig. 1-64). Only when you want a lawn should you apply the material evenly and heavily. Cover all the areas with the glue mixture and ground cover or you'll be left with bald spots.

You can fix rocks in some areas by applying diluted glue over them (fig. 1-79). More dilute matte medium sprayed over the synthetic grass and bushes from a sprayer will further seal the ground cover to the trainboard (fig. 1-80). Be sure that the sprayer has a fine mist setting. Be certain to cover the track and buildings with masking tape. Move into the valley area with the next soil and grass combination

Fig. 1-80. A very fine spray of matte medium will bond everything in place. Cover buildings and track switches to protect them from overspray. Your track will have to be cleaned again after spraying, just as it did after painting.

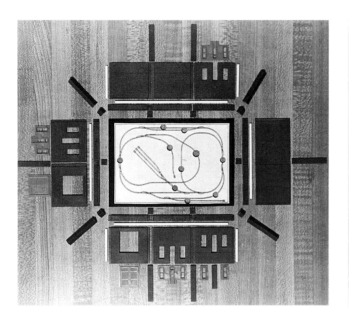

Fig. 1-82. The prefabricated and cut parts for building the Electrical Switch and Industrial Siding Co.

Fig. 1-83. Before final installation check train clearance with an NMRA (National Model Railroad Association) track and clearance gauge.

and then proceed to the east end. Once everything dries, vacuum up any loose material.

The Other Buildings

After the station, we added several other buildings to the Great N-pire Railroad. Walther's Inter-state Fuel and Oil was a logical choice for one industry, as trains, trucks, and automobiles all need gasoline and diesel fuel. Model Power's truck terminal will handle a variety of rail freight destined for the town. Both kits were assembled by following the instructions and then detailing them in the same way as the train station. The aerial photograph in fig. 1-81 illustrates their relative positions on the yard spur. They leave room for the proposed Highline track slated for future expansion.

The Electrical Switch and Industrial Siding Co. that houses the control panel and supplies power to the Great N-pire Railroad is a freelanced building constructed from Design Preservation Models modular wall panel kits and Evergreen strip styrene. This is a "make your own kit" because you need a building of a particular size to accommodate the 3⁷⁄16" x 5⅛" control panel that becomes the roof. If this is your first try at the art of freelance kitbashing and scratchbuilding, don't fret over not having a formal set of plans to go by. After cutting the parts to the required lengths, assembly is no different from putting together the other models you have completed. Much of model railroading is freelancing and designing what you want or need.

First assemble all the parts listed in Table 1-9 and shown in

Fig. 1-81. An aerial view shows the layout of the switching yard, the asphalt parking lot, the fuel depot, and the freight transfer terminal.

fig. 1-82. Lay out all the parts in a similar fashion. Next, build the structure in subassembly stages, following the building guidelines that DPM packages with each unit set. The most difficult part of building any structure kit is keeping the walls square. But if you don't get everything perfectly square, it may actually enhance the look of the final building!

The block control panel roof is held in place by the sides of the building. Don't glue the roof in—you will need access for additional electrical switches as you progress through the layout expansion phases. Check for proper locomotive and car clearance between the edge of the loading dock and the track by test-fitting the building over the opening before installing it permanently. Use an N scale NMRA (National Model Railroader Association) gauge (fig. 1-83) or a locomotive as a gauge to check

Fig. 1-84. We installed the E.S.&I.S. Co. building over the control panel hole using wet multitextured paint as glue instead of an actual glue, as we used with the train station.

the clearance. You can attach the building as we did, with the station, or by respraying the leveled area with the multitextured paint and pushing the building into the wet paint (fig. 1-84).

Our congratulations! You have built an operating railroad literally from the ground up with industry and commerce to service. In the next chapter you'll add a steam siding with trackside structures, build a town, and increase the population of people and trees. Until the next N-pire Flyer roars through, Adios!

Fig. 1-85. This is what our layout looks like at this stage. We bet yours looks even better!

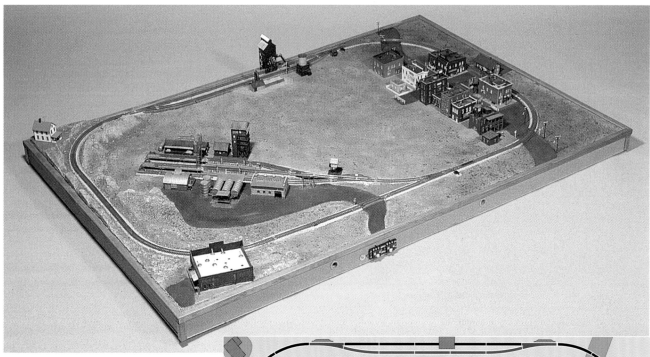

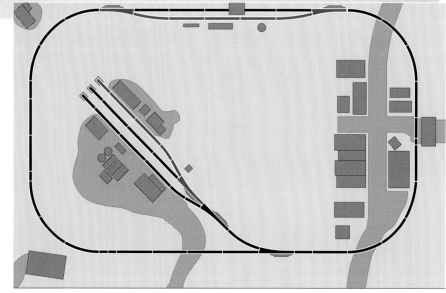

Fig. 2-1. New industrial yard spur and steam siding trackwork for the Great N-pire Railway's Phase 2 expansion is highlighted on a CAD drawing of the layout.

Building the Steam Siding and Main Street

GROWTH COMES QUICKLY for the Great N-pire. So we'll add an inside passing siding to handle the extra rail traffic. It can also be used for fueling steam engines with trackside services (fig. 2-1). The peo- ple who operate our trains, industries, and services need a town to live in. After all, if there weren't a town the railroad would not stop. In this chapter we'll also construct the town of Enville, complete with its Main Street, shops, people, vehicles, and details.

Figure 2-2 shows the modified industrial yard after completion. Since the road gangs were already laying the third spur track, we decided to save the

This view shows all of Enville's Main Street, end to end. You will construct this thriving miniature metropolis in the course of this chapter.

Fig. 2-2. The heart of the expanded switching yard is its electrified track switches, shown here after the trackwork was finished. Switch 1 accesses the left and middle spurs, while switch 2 accesses the new spur.

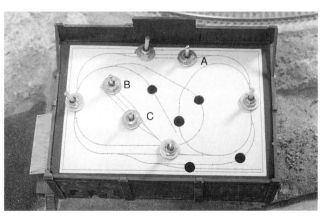

Fig. 2-3. The Electrical Switch and Industrial Siding Co. modified its rooftop control panel with three new DPDT switches for the track's new electrical blocks. DPDT switch A controls power to the steam siding, while DPDT switches B and C are the electrical blocks for the yard and optional spur.

railroad money by immediately installing a few electrical switch machines. The impending Highline track will make conventional switch ground throws difficult to operate, so electrical switch machines are an obvious choice. The convenience of remote switching may entice you to replace every conventional throw on the layout. The Atlas Company has made wiring these elec-

trical switch machines so easy that it would take very little time to change all of them. Be sure to make a decision about this before ballasting the track.

Track plans often evolve over the course of building a layout, and the Great N-pire turns out to be no exception. We initially overlooked the idea of using both outside spur tracks as additional independent electrical track

blocks. In this phase you'll add insulating rail joiners and terminal leads for a new electrical track block on each outer spur. This feature improves two-train operation by creating tracks to park your locomotives. The supplies necessary to accomplish all of this are listed in Table 2-1 under Supplemental Supplies. You wire the electrical blocks in the same way as the first phase, and you'll have to punch two additional holes in the control panel for the electrical DPDT switches (fig. 2-3). This project requires a little time, but you'll be pleased with the additional operation.

It's time to assemble a track crew and get to work expanding the Great N-pire Railroad. The first step is to loosen enough track so you can remove the old switches without bending either the rails or the fragile rail joiners. Using a small pair of pliers, remove the track nails that hold each track section to the roadbed and tabletop. (This is why you used track nails instead of glue and ballast to anchor the track to the roadbed.) In the next chapter you'll remove all track nails permanently after you ballast the track.

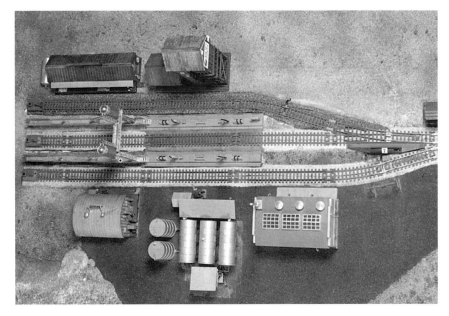

Fig. 2-4. A low-altitude aerial photograph after the yard's completion confirms the length and parallel arrangement of the three yard spurs.

Fig. 2-5. Using a hot glue gun, mount Atlas's slide/push-button electrical switches, which control the electrified switch machines, on the side of the tabletop. The instructions describe how to connect the three color-coded wires to the switches.

Fig. 2-6. Use two different-size jacks to distinguish between the power pack's AC and DC power terminals. This way they can't be confused. The left outlet is the ¼" phone jack for controlling the track's DC train current. The right outlet is a ⅛" jack for powering the electrified switch machines, which use AC current. The two wires from electrical slide switches shown on the right connect inside to the ⅛" outlet.

First, don't forget to spray-paint the track the same color as the main line. With electrified track switches it is important to mask all electrical contacts, including the electric machine itself, before spray-painting. Any extra spray will interrupt the current and prevent the switches from working. Consider painting the switches by hand to ensure that they will operate flawlessly.

Second, lay out the track and use it as a template to mark the tabletop for the roadbed. You did this all previously, so follow the same tracklaying procedure as you did before. The spur should parallel the other two spur tracks and run the same distance (fig. 2-4). To prepare the tabletop for the roadbed, scrape off any excess ground cover. Cut the cork roadbed using the switch pattern shown in the previous chapter. Then glue the roadbed in place, using your marked line as the center line. Now you can insert the insulated rail joiners, add the terminal leads, install the electrified track switches, and nail down the track.

After punching holes through the tabletop for the terminal leads and the electrical switch machine wires, you're ready to wire the electrical switches that will operate the switch machines. Mount the Atlas slide/push-button electrical switch on the side using the hot glue gun (fig. 2-5). Connect the red, green, and black wires according to the instructions and as shown in fig. 2-5. Atlas switch machines use the accessory AC terminals on your power pack,

but your trains use 12-volt DC. To avoid connecting the wrong current from the power pack to the wrong electrical device, use ⅛"-diameter electrical jacks for the AC instead of the ¼" size you used for the track's DC. The jacks are then incompatible and there is no way you can accidentally short out the system (fig. 2-6).

Continued on page 50

TABLE 2-1
Tracklaying Supplies

- 5 pieces 5" straight sections Atlas N scale track no. 2501
- 1 piece 2½" straight section Atlas N scale track no. 2509
- 1 piece half 9¾"-radius section Atlas N scale track no. 2511
- 1 bumper section Atlas N scale track no. 2536
- 1 left-hand remote Atlas N scale track switch no. 2700
- 1 right-hand remote Atlas N scale track switch no. 2701
- 1 right-hand Custom Line Atlas N scale track switch no. 2751
- 2 Caboose ground throws no. 206-S
- 2 strips cork roadbed
- Rail joiners, insulated rail joiners, track nails
- Floquil rail brown spray paint
- 1 Micro DPDT electrical switch, wire, wire nuts
- Tools, including hot glue gun

Supplemental Supplies
- 2 Micro DPDT electrical switches

Fig. 2-7. A view from across the valley highlights the new agricultural buildings—
a co-op grain elevator and transfer building—on the new spur.

Detailing the Yard with Structures

Since the existing yard industries include a rail freight transfer building and a fuel depot, we chose an agriculture-related building for the new siding. Bachmann's co-op elevator, dressed up with Microscale decals, gives a nice vertical dimension to the yard. You could finish the layout after phase 3 with a farming scene and not build the Highline route at all, as agricultural industries are served by rail across the United States. A farmhouse, barn, fields, and farming equipment could be a perfect centerpiece to this layout. On our layout we completed the scene with a long storage and transfer building (fig. 2-7).

To the right of the grain elevator resides a transfer building, which we purchased for 99 cents! It's not uncommon for train stores to take trade-in kits and resell them at low prices. A number of the kits we used on this layout were partially assembled trade-ins. All we did was clean, assemble, paint, weather, decal, and detail them at a lower cost than a new kit. Local and national train shows and swap meets also offer many usable items at low prices.

Decals are important details that can enhance the realistic appearance of any structure. Signs are the details that give your buildings a purpose. They

Fig. 2-8. The first step in decaling is dipping the decal into clean water for 10 seconds. This begins to loosen the decal from its paper.

Fig. 2-9. Place the decal on a damp paper towel for a minute or until it slides freely from the paper backing.

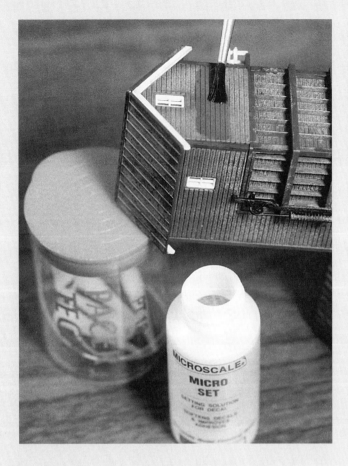

Fig. 2-10 (left). While the decal is loosening, prepare the surface of model where the decal is to be applied by brushing a coat of Micro Set over it.

Fig. 2-11 (above). Now slide the decal off the paper onto the model's surface using your hobby tools. Be careful not to tear the decal.

announce to the world what goes on inside the building, what products are bought and sold. Some signs (decals) are put directly on the building's exterior surface; others need supports created from sheet styrene and painted. It depends upon the type of sign and the building.

Figures 2-8 through 2-13 illustrate the basic steps of decaling. Study and follow the instructions included with each decal sheet. For other kits without instructions, we'll go through the procedure step by step. First cut out the decal from the sheet, trimming the excess film carefully. Dip the decal into clean water for 10 seconds (fig. 2-8), then place it on a damp paper towel (fig. 2-9) for a minute or until the decal slides freely from the paper backing. Never force off a decal—they are fragile and may tear or rip. Next, use a small paintbrush to prep the area on the model

where the decal is to be applied with Micro-Set (fig. 2-10). It's good idea to do all of this in a well-ventilated area.

Now slide the decal off the sheet onto the model and position (fig. 2-11). The decal's position can be gently changed by floating the decal with a little water applied by brush. Once it's in position gently blot off the excess water with a paper towel (fig. 2-12) and carefully apply the Micro-Sol solution with your brush over the decal's entire surface. This solution softens the decal, which allows it to conform to the model's details underneath (fig. 2-13). Any decal given this treatment looks as if it were painted on the structure. This process also makes the decal so soft that it can tear very easily. At this point, you should set the model aside and allow the decal to dry.

After the decal has dried for at least eight hours, give it an

overcoat to seal and protect it. Low humidity can often cause untreated decals to dry up, crack, flake, and disintegrate, producing some interesting but not recommended weathering effects. Microscale offers several overcoat solutions for the final sealing and finishing. Testor's Dullcote and

Table 2-2. Structures

Walthers
• Cornerstone Series, Shady Junction Structures no. 3205

Bachman
• Coaling Station no. 45811
• Diesel Fuel & Sanding Facility no.1516

Lifelike
• Co-op Grain Elevator

Heljan
• Container Transfer Crane no. 665 (Long Transfer Building)

AHM
• Steam Sanding Facility

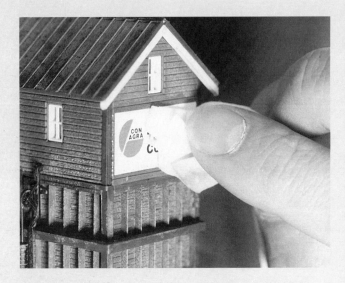

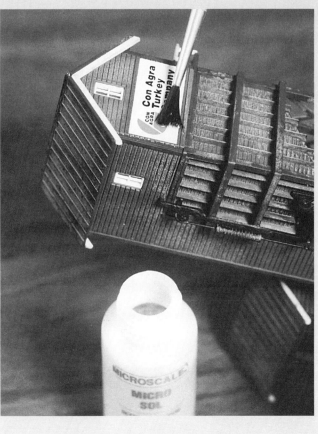

Fig. 2-12. Once it is in position, gently blot off the excess water with a paper towel.

Fig. 2-13. The final step is to apply Micro-Sol solution carefully over the entire decal. Set the model aside and allow the decal to dry. Finish the process as described in the text.

dilute matte medium will also work well.

A dried decal retains a gloss finish that may look out of place on a weathered building with a flat finish. Earlier we discussed how few things in nature have gloss finishes. Overcoats will not only protect the decal but will change the gloss finish to a flat one. Any of these treatments will provide a foundation for weathering or additional painting if required. Signs age and weather just like the exteriors of buildings, but there are exceptions. The type and age of the sign in comparison to the history and current function of a particular building will determine how much weathering you do. Previous weathering treatments may have been altered where the decals were applied. After finishing the decal, weather the afflicted areas again to match the original weathering.

Once you start, you'll find it hard to stop decaling. Go back and add signs to Enville's existing buildings and add them to buildings before installing them on the layout. Don't overdo signing—use some restraint, but use them wherever they make sense.

Walther's elevated watchman's shanty from their lineside structures kit and a kitbashed Bachmann Plus diesel fuel and sanding facility are the last buildings added to the switching yard. The elevated watchman's shanty is a traditional railroad structure with an important function. In addition to the switching, the watchman keeps track (pardon the pun) of the traffic in and out of the yard. The diesel fuel and sanding facility is a logical extension of the fuel depot. Utilize the space between the tracks for this facility. The fuel depot can now handle three types of fuel: gasoline for automobiles, fuel oil for heating homes and businesses, and diesel locomotive fuel for diesel locomotives.

You'll have to modify or kitbash the diesel service facility because of the yard's limited size and length. Combine the two facilities into one by using only half of each kit. Use only two narrow yellow sanding walkways with cutaway handrails (except for the ends), so diesels can receive sand on all three spurs. You'll also have to shorten the elevated walkway between the two sanding towers because of the distance between the tracks. The walkway is not a necessary structure, but it is a nice addition. Change the concrete walkways by gluing the narrow walkways onto the wider walkways. Add four fuel pumps, control panels, and accessories to the medians. Since the yellow on the sanding portion of the facility is much too bright, spray-paint it silver; the fueling portion can remain a concrete gray. Save the remaining parts of the kit for future projects.

Fig. 2-14. Looking down the throat of the switching yard we first see the elevated watchman's shanty, which controls access to the yard. Between the tracks a pair of Union Pacific F7s receive fuel and sand in the new diesel facility. On the left a short freight train of tank cars deliver fuel to the fuel depot. The completed yard is certainly keeping busy!

Fig. 2-15. An eastbound freight on the main line loads coal from the coaling tower as it passes underneath, while a westbound steam engine on the steam siding pauses to take on sand and water.

All that's left is to hard-wire the track blocks to the DPDT electric switches as you have done before. Once everything tests A-OK you can add the industries to the third spur.

Building the Steam Siding

In the days of the iron horse, railroads built their major steam locomotive servicing facilities at terminal yards. In addition, every railroad had refueling stops along each route. Engine yard facilities are too extensive to add to your layout, but a fuel stop is a perfect alternative. Here the engine and tender would replenish water, fuel (wood, coal, or fuel oil), and sometimes sand (fig. 2-15). Water heated by the fuel in the engine's firebox created the steam that powered the locomotive. Sand was used for traction on the rails when an engine was starting from a dead stop, climbing grades with heavy trains, or traveling on slippery rails. Tenders carried fuel and water for the engine, while the sand dome was located on top of the locomotive boiler to keep the sand warm and dry.

Steam siding construction follows the tracklaying principles in the previous section. Table 2-1 lists the track you'll need for both this siding and the third industrial yard spur. If you saved the left-hand manual switch from the industrial yard, you only have to buy a single right-hand manual switch. After removing enough track nails, replace the two straight end sections with the appropriate right and left switches. Complete the siding with the curved sections that came with each switch and three straight sections of track. Follow the established procedure for marking and laying the roadbed and track, then install either ground throws or the electric switch machines. The roadbed won't need painting, since ballast will cover it. After laying the siding, test it and then add the complementary buildings.

Assemble, paint, and weather all three structures before installing them. The coaling tower is a factory-assembled Bachmann structure. You can modify the stairway so that the tower straddles the main line. The water tank and spout are from Walther's lineside structures, the same kit that included the yard's elevated watchman's shanty. Finally, the sanding facility is a kit available from several manufacturers. This kit is a faithful reproduction of the Cumbres and Toltec Scenic Narrow Gauge Railroad facility at Cumbres Pass, Chama, New Mexico. You can alter the kit as we did by reversing the layout of the pieces so that it fits in the designated area.

Create a temporary mock-up of the Shortline loop and the

Fig. 2-16 (left). To ensure enough clearance between the trackwork and steam siding structures, temporarily lay out the trackwork from the phase 3 and 4 expansions, the Shortline and the Highline Oval.

Fig. 2-17 (above). A westbound AT&SF 4-6-2 Pacific takes on all three consumables—sand, coal, and water, from left to right—in one stop on the steam siding. Commuters will appreciate the shortened fueling times of this arrangement.

Highline route as shown in fig. 2-16 to ensure that the structures are positioned correctly. Normally, a coaling tower would be on a siding by itself, where it would not interfere with mainline rail traffic. Since there is not enough room to build an additional siding, center the coaling tower over the second straight section from the east switch. Because of tight clearances, you should be fairly precise when positioning the structure. Check your clearances by using your widest rolling stock. Make sure everything passes by without touching any portion of the stairway or tower.

The water tank and sanding tower are near the coaling tower to simplify the refueling procedure. All steam fueling structures are aligned so that the engine stops once for everything and not at each individual station (fig. 2-17). Of course, this works when a steam engine travels one direction but not in the other. (We

found that we run our trains counterclockwise more than clockwise because of how the yard is laid out.) Diesels are built to operate equally well in either direction. They use this siding as a passing siding, not as a fuel stop.

Now that you have fuel for the trains, you'll build a town for the people of Enville to live in.

Building Enville's Main Street

In the beginning, railroads connected established cities and towns. As the populace expanded westward, towns sprang up along the railroad right-of-way and owed their existence to the railroad. Many a town across the United States had its Main Street next to the tracks. Lordsburg, New Mexico, is one example of many such Western towns (fig. 2-18). In Midwestern towns like Oshkosh, Wisconsin, however, railroad tracks crisscross through the city and along backyards (fig. 2-19).

Choose those buildings that appeal to you, build each of them carefully, then lay out the town to see how the buildings work together as Main Street. Wait until they are all finished before gluing them down. This will give you ample opportunity to alter the position of buildings. You now have the chance to "pave" Main Street. If the result is not what you expected, just tear it up and do it over.

Figure 2-20 is an aerial photograph taken during the initial planning and development phase of Enville. Using the individual building foundations, lay out Main Street to ensure that it will fit inside the proposed Shortline loop and the Highline route, including space for scenery. The 11 buildings for Main Street row are listed in Table 2-3. You can scratchbuild the bakery next to the bank using parts left over from the Electrical Switch and Industrial Siding Plant, but all the other buildings are built from kits. We came upon the 2¾"

Fig. 2-18. A view looking southeast across the Southern Pacific main line and yard toward the Main Street of Lordsburg, New Mexico, which parallels the tracks similar to Enville's. Lordsburg is typical of many American towns that grew up alongside the railroad tracks.

Fig. 2-19. A residential section of Oshkosh, Wisconsin, has an industrial spur operating between backyards and streets. Many Eastern and Midwestern cities have railroads crisscrossing the cityscape, servicing thousands of industries.

street width by placing four vehicles side by side (fig. 2-20). This width allows traffic to flow in both directions and still have parked cars on both sides of the street.

Using Evergreen ¼" sidewalk sheet styrene, construct foundations for buildings without one. Narrow all the sidewalks to one sidewalk square around the building's exterior perimeter. This saves valuable tabletop space by reducing the amount of unusable space between buildings. Be sure to

leave adequate clearance between buildings and the trains moving on the track. Use the NMRA gauge to check clearance between the tailor and the Shortline's turnout track, which you temporarily push-pin in place for reference.

Feel free to add, remove, substitute, or change the number or type of buildings; after all, it is your town and the choices are yours. A large selection of downtown buildings is available from numerous manufacturers.

The only consideration is that everything fits into the allotted space inside all the track lines and scenicked areas.

Interior Structure Details

Miniature buildings that are supposed to be real need more than what is included in the box. This subject is too large to address here, but Kalmbach Publishing Co. offers several fine books on the subject. If you're interested, here are a few points to consider about interiors and exteriors.

First, avoid empty-looking buildings. Many modelers use pieces of thin cardboard as view blocks, staggering them in patterns to give the effect of interior rooms. View blocks also keep you from seeing into an empty building and out another window. In combination with window decorations, this partitioning is effective, but the rooms are dark and still look vacant. We offer a different solution.

Besides the motion of the trains, miniature lights are perhaps the most enchanting detail you can add to any layout. Once again, this is simple to do and requires only a little advance preparation. Believe it or not, you will have one up on many pros and old timers in this hobby who simply do not bother to take the time to light their structures.

Where do you obtain inexpensive miniature lights? For the price of one or two "hobby" bulbs you can purchase a string of miniature Christmas tree lights! We bought a string of 50 for $2.99 at our local craft store. These lights produce just the right amount of illumination, they do not overheat, and they are long lasting and replaceable.

Interior lights require certain building modifications. The first is

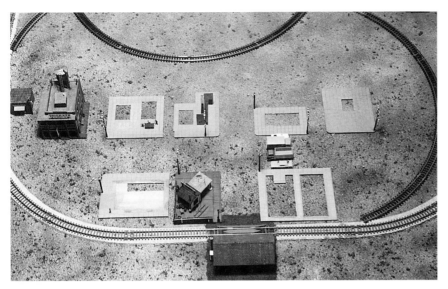

Fig. 2-20. This oblique aerial photograph shows the initial Main Street planning of Enville. Use building foundations with sidewalks to block out the area each individual building will require. A single strip of buildings (like Lordsburg in fig. 2-18) with a Main Street in front would fit in the space as well.

to eliminate any building glow. Model building walls are solid but translucent because they are molded plastic. Most interior walls need a coat of black paint, especially if the exterior is molded in a light color. Of course, if you can see the black walls through large windows paint them again after the black paint has dried. Fill all seams between front, back, and side walls with glue and paint, strip styrene, or opaque tape. Similarly, glue a styrene strip along the base of the wall and the foundation to prevent light leaks under the walls. Figure 2-21 demonstrates the step-by-step process that prepares a building's interior for illumination.

Now for the windows. After glazing the windows with clear styrene, the next step is to make curtains! Curtains can be as simple as a strip of paint across the back side of the clear styrene or as intricate as Detail Associates' etched brass venetian blinds. White drafting tape works well for shades, as does the sticky edge of yellow 3M Post-it Notes

covered by transparent tape. Even the blue striped paper on the packages of Microscale decals make wonderful vertical curtains. Just remember to vary the height of the curtains from window to window for that "lived-in" look.

What can you do to model what goes on inside? We stumbled

upon a really cute solution from some German kits, which often include paper window dressings. Everyone gets those small stamps in the mail from record and video clubs, right? If you examine these stamps, you'll find that N scale people are printed on many of them. Cut them out, align them across the back of the window below the curtain line, and tape them in place. Your buildings now have instant interior scenes. Other scenes and patterns can be cut from magazines, but be sure to erase any printing on the back of a paper cutout by gentle sanding against a very fine grade of sandpaper. In fig. 2-22 the miniature Woolworth's five and dime store has window decorations. Make styrene window boxes and insert thin sheet styrene flats with printed paper cutouts glued to them. You should glue paper to styrene with a glue similar to Weldbond Glue, because normal white glue won't hold.

All of this seems to be a lot of work, but remember there is no pressure on you to do it all. You

Table 2-3. Main Street Structures

Company	Kit Designation	Enville's Main Street Shop
Bachman	Randolph's Restaurant no. 35151 . . .	Drugstore and Cafe
	Engine # 9 Firehouse no. 35153	Firestation
Model Power	Railroad Hotel no. 1512	Trailblazer Hotel
Design Preservation Models	Crickett's Saloon no. 511	The Hot Spot
	Bruce's Bakery no. 501	Pool Hall, Barber Shop
	Corner Apothecary no. 507	Union Bank
	Otto Parts no. 503	Woolworth's Five and Dime
Scratchbuilt from DPM Parts		Saul's Bakery
Walthers Cornerstone Series	University Avenue Shops no. 3208 . .	Quality Tailors and Laundry
	University Avenue Shops no. 3208 . .	Superior Hardware
Micro Engineering	40's Gas Station no. 65139	Mobil Gas Station

Fig. 2-21. If you use interior lights, you have to deal with every building's interior and windows. First, darken all walls to prevent them from glowing. Paint the interior walls flat black if necessary. Next, cover the windows with clear styrene glued at the corners and create window shades with 3M Post-it Notes or tape. Finally, tape a miniature picture from a magazine or advertisement as an interior view, as described in the text.

Fig. 2-22. Evening falls upon some after-work shoppers pausing to admire the displays in Woolworth's magical windows.

may decide that all of this is too much bother, and that is fine. Many experienced modelers build beautiful street scenes without working lights or building interiors.

Exterior Details

Certainly Main Street would look barren if the shops did not have signs hanging over the sidewalk and street. Walthers makes an HO sign kit, and some of the signs are appropriately sized for N scale. A combination of manufactured signs and custom signs made from sheet styrene turns Main Street into an advertiser's dream (fig. 2-23).

The other important visual perspective that modelers often overlook is the view onto rooftops (fig. 2-24). We tower over everything and are forced to assume a bird's-eye view of a layout. Our eyes are drawn to rooftops.

Roofs contain all kinds of devices, from skylights to water tanks, for the comfort and business of the people inside. Piping by itself is a bewildering array that includes stove pipes, vent pipes for air and plumbing, and pipes that curve over and connect to telephone and electrical wires. Roof access is provided by ladders, fire escapes, roof hatches,

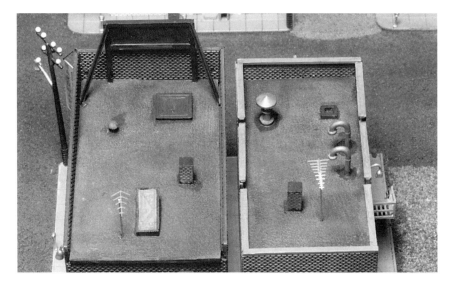

Fig. 2-24. Like Gulliver in Lilliput, model railroaders are always looking down on our creations; so roof details are an important addition, which most manufacturers neglect. Add them for a tremendous increase in realism.

Fig. 2-23. Across the tracks Enville's Main Street is a thriving, bustling community.

cellar-style slanted doors, and outhouse-like cubicles leading from inside staircases. Even bits of small junk find their way onto dusty dirty weathered rooftops.

The rooftops in Enville are from kit stock. Alter them with stripping for seams, sandpaper for texture, and scribed styrene to create different appearances. Paint all with a weathered black and spray them with Testor's Dullcote. Construct the roof apparatus from extra kit pieces: sprues, sheet styrene, and small parts, as well as round, tubular, rod, and square stock. Air-conditioning units are nothing more than two wood crates. Glue them together and paint them silver.

Installing Main Street

Now that the buildings are constructed, it's time to survey Main Street from the air. First out-line the building foundations, Main Street itself, connecting highways, and alleys (fig. 2-25). Get the road crews ready to pave the roads. Apply the Main Street surface using the same techniques as you used for the asphalt parking lot around the fuel depot and truck transfer building. First remove all brush and turf by scraping. Spread a thin layer of finely ground asphalt over dilute matte medium solution brushed onto the tabletop. Once it dries, vacuum up the excess asphalt. Weather the road by rubbing it with your fingers. This lightens and streaks the gray unevenly (fig. 2-26).

Next, call the Enville Electric Co. for help with the electrical underground cable to wire all of the interior lights. Punch holes through the foam-core tabletop, widen them to approximately ¼", and insert a Christmas tree

light through each. A drop of Weldbond will hold each lamp in place with tape securing the wiring underneath (fig. 2-27). Do not cut off the extra lights yet, as you may need more elsewhere on the Great N-pire Railroad. Run some of these extra lights to the structures around the industrial yard.

Now position each Main Street shop onto its base. If you are lighting your buildings, check for light leaks by using a penlight. Seal any cracks with paint or strip styrene, then glue each structure into its respective outline. Seal any cracks between the foundations and the ground with an edging of matte medium and ground cover. It may take time to cover cracks between the foundation and the ground, but the results are worth the effort. Remember, you want the buildings to look as if their foundations

Fig. 2-25. After finishing the exterior and interior details of the buildings, continue laying out Main Street. Mark the outlines of the building foundations in preparation for paving the street.

Fig. 2-26. Main Street's paving was done in the same way as the fuel depot's parking lot during the Great N-pire's initial construction.

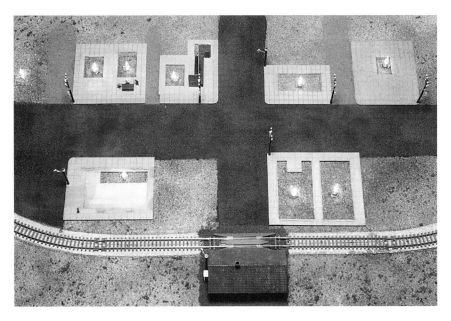

Fig. 2-27. Lights! Camera! Action! Enville Electric Power Company's underground wiring for Main Street's lights is a success! Each foundation had rectangular cutouts in the floor for installing lights. Inside each cutout punch ¼" holes through the foam-core tabletop for a single Christmas tree light.

continue into the ground as real foundations do.

Sidewalk and Street Details

Besides shops, city streets have sidewalk and street details. They include everyday items like mailboxes, trash cans, benches, telephone poles, street lamps, hydrants, parking meters, telephone booths, bicycle racks, fire call boxes, traffic signs, billboards, and alley junk like crates, trash bins, and tires. All of these details are available from a variety of manufacturers and add to the realism of the street scene. Almost anything you can think of on a real street is available as a casting or can be scratchbuilt.

Populating Enville

Generally, model railroads appear to be underpopulated. If you drive around your own town you may see very few people about except for certain areas, times of day, or special occasions. In fact many towns today look empty because most work is done indoors. If you replicate this in a model railroad town, it ends up looking like a ghost town. To make Enville look right, consider having almost every figure out and about, doing something. We used between 40 and 50 figures on Main Street alone, and it could use a few more.

Painted people are available, but they can be expensive. One of the better bargains is a box of 120 unpainted Preiser figures. Painting these figures usually requires a magnifying glass or an Optivisor, a 3/0 brush, and good paints. Water-base paint works best on the type of plastic that Preiser uses for castings. Figure-painting is a perfect filler when you are short of time but want to

Fig. 2-28. An eastbound freight moves past downtown Enville. All of your hard work certainly pays off—compare this completed view of Main Street to the barren view at the beginning of this chapter.

make some progress on your layout. You need only 10 or 15 minutes to paint a figure, and these segments will add up.

Bachmann and Model Power also offer painted people. They are less expensive, but they do not come in as many different poses as the Preiser figures. When you're populating Main Street and elsewhere, create mini-scenes with several people at a time. Two people having a conversation, parents and children looking in a shop window, work crews loading goods or changing a flat tire—these are ideas from real life. As you look through the accompanying photographs you will find many of these scenes.

Automobiles and trucks are the last detail to add at this stage. There are essentially two types: vehicles that have injection-molded shells with windows, and those that are solid cast and have painted windows.

Some vehicles are slightly undersized, and others are oversized. Often this is not an issue until you put an underscaled car or truck next to an oversized one, and then the difference becomes very noticeable. This also applies to painted versus clear windows. You can mix different brands and types, but you must do it carefully. We chose solid cast vehicles for the most part and integrated the casting of several different manufacturers by keeping them separated on the layout (fig. 2-28).

All this work with Enville should keep you busy for some time, but there is no reason to hurry through it or stop running trains. Enjoy it! You may even jump to the next phase before finishing Main Street. In the real city you live in, buildings are always being constructed, torn down, and rebuilt. Cities grow, Enville will too.

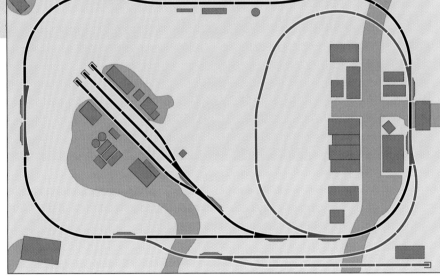

Fig. 3-1. This is the CAD drawing of the Great N-pire layout in the third expansion phase, which adds the passing siding, freight spur, and Shortline Loop.

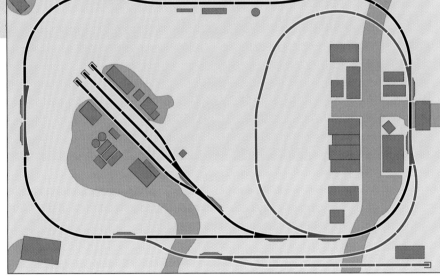

Building the Passing Siding, Freight Spur, and Shortline Loop

STAGE 3

LAYING TRACK switches is a major part of the work in this phase. You'll need a minimum of four switches, two for the Highline Loop and two for the Shortline. We initially planned to use a pair for the passing siding and a pair for the interior loop known as the Shortline Oval, bringing the design total to four. Then we decided to add a freight spur onto the passing

Fig. 3-2. A pair of Union Pacific F3s hauls a colorful freight through Enville past the pine grove on the outskirts of town.

Fig. 3-3. These are the Highline Loop access switches installed back to back on the west end of the layout. If you install them now, you can ballast all the track on the layout.

Fig. 3-4. Locate and install the passing siding's west end switch on the proper side of the insulated rail joiners to the left of the ground throw. The switch is on a slope, so elevate the ground throw on three cut pieces of cork roadbed painted gray to look like concrete.

siding, which increased the total by one. Having this specific freight spur will allow you to add a connecting track to attach the Great N-pire to another layout or to an extension of this layout (fig. 3-1).

We also decided to install the Highline Loop's access switches at this time (fig. 3-3). It became clear that by including the Highline switches we could ballast the track now instead of at the end of the project. There is plenty of work left to do. We designed the Great N-pire to be flexible, of course, so you can stop at any point in the track

plan, disregard additional loops, sidings, and spurs, and ballast the remaining track.

There is nothing new about laying the track. You are an old pro at it by now, but there are some areas that you still need to consider. Pay close attention to how you replace the existing straight track section on the east side of the insulated rail joiners with the passing siding switch. Be sure to exchange the switch on the correct side of the insulated joiners. You don't want to interfere with the existing electrical block on the west end (fig. 3-4).

This passing siding switch is on an elevated roadbed which itself is inclined to reach the Indian Bluffs. This means that the added passing siding sections must rise from tabletop level to meet the switch. Additionally, you'll have to stack some cut sections of roadbed and glue them underneath for the Caboose Hobbies' ground throw. The track foreman will have to post a slow-speed-limit sign in front of the passing siding's S curve, which is between the turnout and the road crossing. This curve became known as Deadman's Curve because of the number of derailments at high speeds. It is very dangerous for engineers—it is not only S-shaped, but it is on an incline and crosses a road.

Install a Kadee magnetic coupler on the 2½" straight section of the passing siding east of the road crossing. Modify this coupler the same way you did on the nearby main line. This uncoupler allows switchers to uncouple cars, spot them on either the passing siding or the freight spur, do a run-around using the main track, pick them up from the other end, and take them to their destination.

TABLE 3-1. Tracklaying Supplies

• 8 pieces 5" straight sections Atlas N scale track no. 2501
• 2 pieces 2½" straight sections Atlas N scale track no. 2509
• 1 piece 1¼" straight section Atlas N scale track no. 2509
• 1 piece ¾" straight section Atlas N scale track no. 2509
• 1 piece 19"-radius curved section Atlas N scale track no. 2526
• 4 pieces half 9¾"-radius curved sections Atlas N scale track no. 2511
• 11 pieces 9¾"-radius curved sections Atlas N scale track no. 2510
• 4 right-hand Custom Line Atlas N scale track switches no. 2751
• 3 left-hand Custom Line Atlas N scale track switches no. 2750
• 7 Caboose ground throws no. 206-S
• 1 Kadee magnetic uncoupling ramp
• 5 strips cork roadbed
• Rail joiners, insulated rail joiners, track nails
• Floquil rail brown spray paint
• 3 Micro DPDT electrical switches, wire, wire nuts
• Evergreen strip styrene
• Tools including soldering gun and hot glue gun

Continued on page 64

Fig. 3-5. A Heinz 57 billboard reefer is cut out from the main line and left on the freight siding for unloading. Because of the siding's close proximity to the main line it shares the same salt-and-pepper ballast.

Ballasting Trackwork

Assemble the ballasting materials listed in Table 3-2. You can purchase both the little squeeze bottle and the small sprayer in the cosmetics-pharmaceutical section of a supermarket. Fill the sprayer with a 1:1 mix of isopropyl alcohol and water, and prepare a mixture of ⅓ alcohol, ⅓ matte medium, and ⅓ water

for the squeeze bottle. This mixture will be the ballast bonding agent or glue. Fold the index card in half and tape one end shut, so you can use it to spread the ballast onto the tracks and roadbed.

Prototype ballast comes in different colors and materials depending upon each railroad's preference, the availability of certain rocks, and the geographic location. Some railroads use one type and color of ballast on the main line and a different color on the sidings or branch lines. Many roads use a gray ballast for their main lines—our local Southern Pacific is one of them. If you are in doubt about which color to use, you can't go wrong with gray. We decided to use a warm buff-colored limestone ballast from Arizona Rock and Mineral Co. on the track in the Indian Bluffs. This color resembles our base earth

color and looks as if the ballast were mined from the local area (fig. 3-13, page 64). In the industrial switching yard we used the same ballast, which we stained brown with a wash of brown ink and alcohol (fig. 3-14, page 64). We used a contrasting salt-and-pepper-colored ballast for the Mainline and Highline Loop. The three colors complemented the landscape around them and enhanced the impression of distance from one geographic locale to another. Remember, this is your railroad—don't be afraid to exercise your own judgment.

Put a small amount of ballast into the folded index card and pour a mound of it down the middle of the track and along the roadbed (fig. 3-6). Next, spread the ballast, using a paintbrush to fill the gaps between the ties (fig. 3-7). Be careful not to push the

Table 3-2
Ballasting Supplies

- N scale ballast
- Index card
- Small soft paintbrush no. 3 to no. 7
- Small squeeze bottle for glue mixture
- Small sprayer for alcohol
- 70 percent isopropyl rubbing alcohol
- Matte medium
- Water

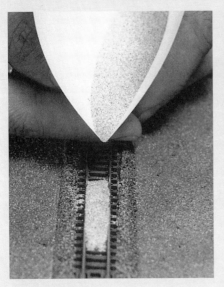

Fig. 3-6. Use a folded and taped index card to pour the ballast onto the track.

Fig. 3-7. Spread the ballast evenly using a camel-hair brush. Fill the space between the ties and along the sides of the cork roadbed. Be careful not to push the ballast up against the inside of the rails.

Fig. 3-8. Dampen the ballast by misting it with a 1:1 solution of alcohol and water from a small pump sprayer. Wetting the ballast first will prevent it from clumping when you apply the bonding agent.

ballast up against the inside of the rails. It will take a little practice to get the hang of using a brush to smooth out the ballast, but once you do, you'll find it easy. Our advice is to be gentle—it does not take much effort to push the ballast around with a brush. Now use the same brushing technique on the sides of the roadbed. In model railroading the cork roadbed is used as substrate or foundation for the track and ballast. The illusion it presents is that the elevated track is supported by a roadbed of solid ballast. Real railroad main lines are well maintained and manicured to handle the traffic load.

After you have groomed the ballast, dampen it thoroughly with the alcohol/water in the spray bottle by gently misting the mixture over the ballast (fig. 3-8). Spraying the ballast settles the particles in place and prepares them for the bonding agent. If you skip this step the flow from the squeeze bottle will move the ballast out of position and make it clump into unrealistic puddles. The final step is to flood the area with the bonding agent, using the small squeeze bottle (fig. 3-9).

The alcohol helps the evaporation process by drying the bonding agent faster.

Take special care when ballasting around switches. N scale switches are delicate machines, and ballasting can easily prevent them from working. Ground throws and switch rails may not close because of interference from ballast particles, poor electrical contact from rail section to rail section may occur because the bonding agent has insulated the metal, and even the electric switch machines may fail to operate.

A number of experienced modelers will not risk ballasting switches at all. They value smooth operation of their rolling stock through the switches over appearance. There are several alternatives to consider: you can paint the cork roadbed the same color as your ballast, ignore it altogether, or spread a very fine ballast layer, enough to cover the cork surface. We recommend painting or lightly ballasting the

cork under each switch by lifting up it, then ballasting the edges of the roadbed alongside the track. This should trick any viewer's eye and eliminate electrical and mechanical problems. Be sure not

Fig. 3-10. Construct Main Street's railroad track and road crossing from sections of cut roadbed glued between the tracks.

Fig. 3-9. Flood the ballast with the alcohol, water, and matte medium bonding agent using a small squeeze bottle. When dry, the ballast will hold the track in place, allowing you to remove the track nails.

to spray or flood around any track switch, especially the electrical machines or electrical contact points. Use eyedroppers instead of the sprayer and squeeze bottle for both wetting and gluing the ballast—eyedroppers are much more controllable. Whatever you do, be careful, or you can undo a lot of hard work.

Another place to avoid ballast is at road crossings. At each crossing extend the road across the tracks in the same way as real roads cross tracks. Lay extra cork roadbed between tracks that are close together to create a road base (fig. 3-10), and spread the asphalt mixture over the top. This forms a raised road between the main line and passing siding. Construct asphalt road ramps from tabletop to track level, using the same technique as you used for ballast. Shape a pile of loose asphalt into a ramp using the same brush you used on the ballast. Then spray it with the alcohol solution before saturating it with the bonding

Fig. 3-11. An Enville resident in his car waits at a wig-wag for the inevitable freight on the freshly asphalted road crossing. Note the wood strips for the between-the-rail crossing.

agent. Correct any unevenness by a second application.

Ballasting is fun and not as time-consuming as you might think, especially if you can get one other person to help. The two of us did the entire layout in a single evening without any prior practice. Allow the bonding agent to dry overnight and then vacuum up any residue. Once the bonding agent is dry, the track is held in place by the ballast and glue

mixture so you can remove all the track nails. What a difference these two things make! You might want to go around the track and fill in the nail holes. Options for filling the holes include a glue-paint mixture, a ballast and glue mixture, a small pebble, or a track nail minus its round head. Filling in the holes is a detail that's well worth the extra effort—after all, real railroad track doesn't have a hole in the middle of the ties.

Fig. 3-12. A throw-arm extension (made from strip styrene) makes the ground throw near the Enville Depot more accessible. Don't forget to paint it black!

Fig. 3-13. An English 4-4-0 touring cross-country pauses over the Kaibab limestone ballast used for the trackage across the Indian Bluffs.

The location of the passing siding switch next to Enville's Depot made it difficult to get our big fingers in there to operate it. We added a strip styrene throw-arm extension to the switch's extended lever on one end and to the ground throw on the other end by drilling holes in the strip ends with a hobby pin vise. Make the extension long enough to clear the rear of the Depot (fig. 3-12). Don't forget to paint it black. (Our extension remained white so it would photograph well.)

The roadbed supporting the Highline Loop access switches in the Indian Bluffs may need some fill or excavation underneath because the roadbed was originally built for straight sections of track, not switches. You can add roadbed, Sculptamold, or a combination of both if you prefer. You may also have to excavate some of the bluff embankment so that the switch ground throws fit. Sculpt level areas into the Indian Bluffs where the track turns out from the switches and starts the Highline Loop.

Now that you've attended to the track details, you can finish wiring the electrical track blocks and test each one. Assuming that everything checks out A-OK, you can finish the trackwork with ballast. You'll be impressed with the overall improvement in appearance that ballasting brings to your trackwork and how finished the layout will look.

Creating Trees

Take a moment to look out a window. Other than the sky and clouds, what is the prominent feature of the natural landscape that you see, even in the busiest of cities? The answer is trees.

Fig. 3-14. Ballast in the ever-busy switching yard shows its age by the brown staining from rust, dirt, and grime. The color comes from brown india ink and alcohol.

Table 3-3. Tree Supplies

- Natural twigs or cast-metal armatures
- Lichen
- Woodland Scenics foliage net
- Woodland Scenics ground turf
- Caspia
- Candytuft
- Yarrow
- Bamboo sishkebab skewers
- Scenic flocking and used dish-soap container
- Scouring pad
- German pine tree kits
- Testor's military medium green spray paint
- Super glue
- Ultra-hold hair spray

Take a close look at them. They are like snowflakes—no two are the same. They come in many different shapes, sizes, and colors. Generally, trees come in green, except in fall, when yellows, oranges, reds, and russets prevail.

Trees are also the most noticeable scenic element of a model railroad. When we think of the countless layouts we've seen, the pikes with great-looking trees are the most memorable. Sadly, trees often lack realistic appearance. Most of us are victims of what we term the coloring book syndrome—trees are straight brown trunks with round green balls on top. As railroad modelers we know the differences between an American 4-4-0 and an SD-40, but can we describe the difference between an oak and an elm? The subtle bends of the trunk, bark texture, branching pattern, and leaf shape and color are the characteristics that differentiate maples from palms and aspens from firs.

Most layouts, even small ones, require many trees. Don't despair, there is hope—you can buy them, find them, and build them. We'll teach you ways to produce basic trees, whether you build them from kits or from scratch. You can then adapt the techniques to create specific trees indigenous to your railroad's locale. We'll teach you how to modify premade trees to create a more realistic appearance. There are fast ways to make plenty of trees that we will introduce you to, and of course, there are tricks to get around, or in this case through, the forests you may have to plant.

Basic Tree Construction

Model trees in their simplest construction have two parts: the trunk with branches and the

Fig. 3-15. A Santa Fe switcher cuts out a string of freight cars onto the passing siding through a grove of trees near the edge of town. These trees were built as described in figs. 3-16 and 3-17.

Fig. 3-16. On the left is a commercial tree cast in soft metal. Create its three-dimensional shape by bending and twisting the branches into the desired position. The tree on the right is scratchbuilt of twigs that have been cut and glued into the chosen shape. Note that you can make both trees into the same shape.

Fig. 3-17. Model trees consist of two parts: the trunk and branch structure shown at left, and the foliage material that represents the smaller leaves. Make this type of tree with a natural twig trunk and branch assembly foliated with Woodland Scenics foliage netting.

Fig. 3-18. Lichen is one of the classic natural plant materials, used for trees since the dawn of model railroading. Its fine tubular branching sections that become finer and finer make it an ideal choice for representing model treetops.

Fig. 3-19. Woodland Scenics foliage netting is one of the modern synthetic materials that works extremely well as clumps of tree boughs and leaves. See fig. 3-15 for a color picture of these finished trees.

foliage. Commercial and hand-built trees follow the same construction pattern. The trunk and major branches delineate the tree's three-dimensional shape. A fibrous material, glued to the larger branches, defines the tree's final shape. Leaf foliage material glued to the boughs is the last element of your scale model tree.

The trunk materials of commercial trees are cast flat in soft metal or plastic. They are more costly than scratchbuilt trees, which use natural materials or a wire armature for a trunk. Natural trunk material includes twigs, small branches, weeds, decorative plants, or doweling, which are available at art and craft stores (figs. 3-15 to 3-17).

Natural and manmade materials are also suitable for making smaller branches and boughs. The plant most often used for model trees is lichen, a type of plant that lacks stems and leaves. Lichen's tubular branching structure makes it an ideal tree material that is always available at your local train or hobby store. Manmade tree materials include foliage, netting material, and dish scouring pads. These materials provide an interlaced webbing resembling tree branches. When stretched, clumped, teased, painted, and dusted the effect is quite realistic (figs. 3-18 to 3-20).

Leaf material can be any particulate matter that gives the appearance of leaves—ground foam, dyed sawdust, minute paper punches, glitter, or flocking. Try gluing foliage to the tree by dusting it with aerosol hair spray, which acts as a glue for the fine leaf particles. If you desire fruit trees, several scenery companies offer miniature fruit. In fact, an orchard planted with rows of fruit

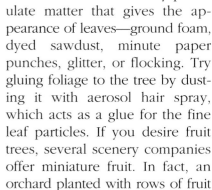

Fig. 3-20. Ordinary household scouring pads available at your local supermarket make excellent pine boughs after being torn into smaller circular pieces, creased, and finished with a dusting of leaf material.

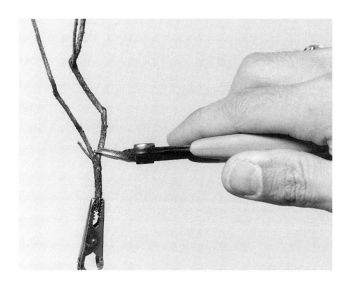

Fig. 3-21. After selecting an appropriate twig for a tree trunk, the first step is to change the length of the twig limbs by cutting the twig off just above the branching nodal point.

Fig. 3-22. Next cut off the extra length of the twig below the upper branching point.

trees uses up the same space on a layout as a forest, but requires far fewer trees (fig. 3-28).

The hobbyist needs only two different tree styles for model railroad layouts—leaf-bearing or deciduous trees and evergreens or pine trees. Both use many of the same materials, only in a different manner. The methods and techniques are interchangeable, providing a variety of different trees. Your first consideration in making trees should be the type of trees you want and where they should go. You don't have to create a tree that is precisely correct to the smallest detail—the way you work with locomotives and rolling stock—but the general shape, size, color, and texture is important.

The location of trees is important too. You can use a small oak as a young oak if it's near the front of a layout, and as an old oak if you place it at the back. You have to find a visual balance when creating and planting trees, as you do with everything else on a model railroad. You achieve this balance by studying nature and by trying things out on your layout. Trees grow where there

is an adequate supply of what they need to sustain themselves. Choose and plant the sizes and varieties of your trees carefully.

Building Deciduous Trees

Try a common tree, *Treei modelus genericus,* first. To start, accumulate suitable trunk and branch material. This is not as hard as some model builders have

made it out to be. Train your eye to look at things as miniature versions of real objects. When you're outside, whether hiking or walking the dogs, look at trees, bushes, twigs, and weeds with an eye tuned to N scale.

Nature does a fine job in replicating big trees with twigs, but there is one important difference; twig limbs are too long between the branching points or nodes to

Fig. 3-23. Then glue the modified branch back in position.

Fig. 3-24. Cut and glue from branch to branch, up and around the entire tree, until the tree has acquired the shape you desire.

Fig. 3-25. Stretch, tease, and glue lichen boughs into position on the branches until you get the full three-dimensional shape of the tree.

Fig. 3-26. As a final step, spray the tree with hair spray and dust it with Woodland Scenics turf material for leaves.

represent a realistic tree. Shortening this branch length is the secret to creating realistic trees. To create a tree skeleton from a twig, cut a short length out of the branches and glue the ends back together (figs. 3-21 to 3-24). Be sure to leave a little extra trunk for "planting" into the tabletop. Repaint the entire altered tree if necessary.

The tree trunk frame is now ready for lichen or another ma-terial. Use appropriately colored lichen in small clumps. You can see the branches and trunks of real trees because the leaves are arranged in clusters. You can also see the sky through trees because trees are not a single mass but a composite of different pieces. Attach the clumps to the branches by dipping the trunk into matte medium before applying the lichen, or by gluing each clump in several locations as you stretch and tease it into place (fig. 3-25).

The final step is to dust the lichen with the leaf matter. The easiest method is to use extra-hold hair spray as described earlier (fig. 3-26). You can sprinkle the foliage on with your fingers or shake it on with a shaker. Don't worry if your first trees are not what you want—nature does-n't make perfect trees, either. Don't throw them away, because you can use them as background trees. The difference between foreground and background trees is in the additional trunk and branch details. To build a common tree as a background tree, you won't need to cut and reat-tach the trunk and branches. Just add the lichen and dust it with the leaf material. Using more detailed trees in front and common trees in the background and forest interiors will help you cover layout areas quickly.

There are still other ways to build trees. Many art and craft stores now stock dried plant materials for interior decoration (fig. 3-27). These dried plants make even better model trees. The most useful plants for N scalers are yarrow, candytuft, and caspia. Caspia can be used to make evergreens. You might be able to find them growing wild, but if they don't grow in your area, visit your local store. Yarrow is a favorite among pro-fessional architectural model builders. Architects like it because it is readily available and looks like a stylized tree. Cutting off the seed heads reveals an excellent branching structure. Cut it off, reattach it, fill it with foliage and leaf material, and you've created a splendid scale tree. Candytuft, also known as sugar bush and pepper grass, is a great plant that makes excellent trees with little work. Look for the dried bunches

Fig. 3-27. Three decorative plants useful in making scale trees can be found in craft stores. From left to right they are yarrow, candytuft, and caspia. Yarrow makes good-looking tree trunks and branches, candytuft is a choice material for small branches with leaf clusters, and caspia makes realistic pine boughs.

that have been left in their natural color, rather than the dyed bunches. There are two different dried preparations of this plant: one with large oval leaves, which is more suitable to larger scales, and the other with smaller leaflets, dyed after the casings have flowered. The latter is more suited for N scale. Choice branchings of candytuft need only painting and planting to create a fine aspen, beech, or birch tree. You can also use candytuft leaf clusters as foliage boughs on other hand-built trunks and branches. Figure 3-29 shows four different deciduous trees made with the preceding methods.

Building Evergreens

Now turn your attention to building an evergreen, *Pinus miniaturii*. You may notice a lack of pine trees in the photographs accompanying this section of the book. Our version of the Great N-pire will look more attractive if we complete the transition from low ground to mountains by using deciduous trees in the valleys with a few pines continued up the mountainside. We'll cover four different pine trees: the bottle-brush spruce, the scouring-pad evergreen, the caspia conifer, and the German Tannenbaum.

The bottle-brush spruce is one of the fastest-growing pines (figs. 3-30 to 3-34). We built two dozen in an hour one night. Bottle-brush spruces are modified from inexpensive premade variety store pine trees that you find for Christmas displays. These trees come in different sizes, which helps create a forest. Using a pair of scissors, trim some branches for a more asymmetrical shape. Color the spruce by spray-painting it. Next spray it with hair spray (even while the paint is wet) and dust it

Fig. 3-28. A closeup photo of the apple orchard ripe with fruit behind the Woolworth's five and dime and between the Shortline Oval and the base of Oro Mountain.

Fig. 3-29. Four different deciduous trees explained in the text. From left to right they are lichen and twig tree, foliage netting and twig tree, yarrow tree with lichen, and orchard tree of candytuft and twigs.

with Woodland Scenics turf. You can vary the shape, colors, and texture in these two stages alone.

Next, flock the tree. Nylon or rayon flocking is found at your local hobby, train, or craft store. If you prep the tree surface with a bonding agent (hair spray again), the fibers will stick to it, giving a realistic pine-needle appearance. Finally, glue on a trunk and plant your tree.

The next two pines start with a tapered dowel. Tapered shishkebab skewers work well without any preparation except cutting them to length. Otherwise round

and taper square balsa wood. Scribe and score the balsa trunk lengthwise with a razor saw to make it look like textured bark. Create evergreen boughs by tearing the scouring pad webbing into thin irregular circular shapes (fig. 3-35). Push these shapes onto the skewer trunk and trim them to a realistic shape. Furnace filters or even sphagnum moss are alternative materials. Finish your tree by spray-painting it, dusting it with foliage or leaf material, and finally flocking it.

The caspia conifer also starts with a shishkebab skewer.

Fig. 3-30. The bottle-brush spruce, as it looks directly from the craft store Christmas display. Use a sturdy pair of scissors to trim some of the bristles, creating boughs and changing the tree's shape from a toylike cone to a more realistic pine-tree shape.

Fig. 3-31. After trimming, spray-paint the spruce an appropriate shade of green. We used Testor's Model Masters brand of military medium green.

Fig. 3-32. A dusting of Woodland Scenics ground turf adds body to the pine boughs and helps to further disguise the bristly toy look.

Randomly glue the caspia to look like weighted boughs (fig. 3-36). Air ferns or certain mosses would also make good branches. All three of these materials are available at art and craft stores. Finish with a coat of spray paint, a dusting of foliage material, and flocking. You can make small pines from caspia alone. Simply choose three tight clumps and trim them all to the same size. Next put them back to back and glue the three stems together with super adhesive to form a single wide trunk. If you bought precolored caspia, the tree is finished. You can dress it up by dusting highlight green over it and painting the trunk or using the other finishing techniques.

The last evergreen is a sectional kit (fig. 3-37) available from several German hobby companies. Originally designed for HO, these pines work extremely well in N scale. Assembly is straightforward, but you can vary the trees by interchanging and swapping the

Fig. 3-35. Constructing a scouring-pad evergreen. After thinning and tearing the scouring pad into a variety of small roughly shaped figures, press each piece onto the dowel and crimp it to look like boughs. The tree then gets the usual paint, dusting, and flock treatment.

Fig. 3-36. Constructing a caspia conifer. Glue each caspia bough to the dowel at an angle to represent a sagging pine bough. After assembly paint, dust, and flock each tree.

Fig. 3-37. The German Tannenbaum before assembly. Each bough section is pegged, with a corresponding socket on the underside. Stack and glue each section from bottom to top. Then comes painting and flocking. You don't have to dust these pines with turf.

Fig. 3-33. Spray the tree with extra-hold hair spray. Then dust scenic flocking over the tree, using a discarded dish-soap container as an applicator. The hair spray acts as a glue, and the flocking looks like pine needles.

Fig. 3-34. The final step is clipping off the wire trunk and base and gluing in a real twig or dowel trunk. Plant the spruce by poking a hole into the foam core or scenery base.

pine bough sections or cutting and gluing in extra branches. These remind us of the classic Tannenbaum or Christmas tree, wouldn't you agree? If you only make a few of each variety, from the bottle-brush spruces to the majestic bough swayers, and intersperse them with some candytuft aspens or birches, you will have created an amazingly realistic forest. You can almost hear the wind whispering through the pines from the freight passing by a small pine grove (fig. 3-38).

Fig. 3-38. A planting of the four different pine trees flanks the main line leading to Enville. From left to right the trees are the scouring-pad evergreen, the caspia conifer, the bottle-brush spruce, and the German Tannenbaum.

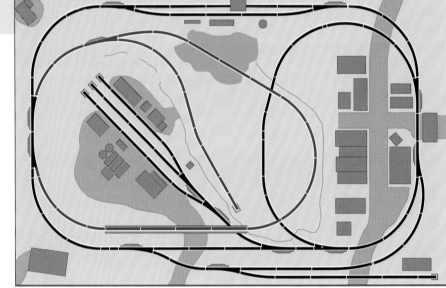

Fig. 4-1. Use this Highline Loop CAD drawing and the matching photograph to lay out the track for the Oro Mountain Loop and Mining Spur. Clearance is important where the Loop crosses the existing track.

STAGE 4

The Highline Loop and Mine Spur

THE FIRST STEP toward finishing your project is to temporarily assemble the Highline Loop from the track listed in Table 4-1. Study and follow the CAD Highline track plan in fig. 4-1 and the corresponding aerial photograph. Proper track height and alignment are critical for Oro Mountain's Highline Loop.

Your tallest, widest, and longest piece of railroad equipment must have enough clearance to pass underneath the last span of the Warren Truss bridge, as shown in fig. 4-3, and through the viaduct that crosses the Shortline. An Atlas 40-foot flatcar with trailers is an excellent height gauge. Because it is one of the tallest cars available, if it clears, your fleet of boxcars, tank cars, flats, reefers, gondolas, and hoppers will too. A taller, wider, or

Table 4-1
Tracklaying Supplies

- 5 pieces 5" straight sections Atlas N scale track no. 2501
- 11 pieces 9¾"-radius curved sections Atlas N scale track no. 2510
- 3 pieces half 9¾"-radius curved sections Atlas N scale track no. 2511
- 1 piece 19"-radius curved section Atlas N scale track no. 2526
- 1 piece 2½" straight section Atlas N scale track no. 2509
- 2 pieces 1¼" straight sections Atlas N scale track no. 2509
- 1 right-hand Custom Line Atlas N scale track switch no. 2751
- 1 Caboose Industries ground throw no. 206-S
- 1 Kadee magnetic uncoupling ramp
- 2 Atlas viaduct kits
- 4 Atlas N scale bridge kits (We used 1 plate girder and 3 Warren truss)
- 1 Atlas N scale bridge piers (risers)
- Rail joiners, insulated rail joiners, track nails
- Floquil rail brown spray paint
- 2 Micro DPDT electrical switches, wire, wire nuts
- Soldering gun, solder, flux
- Usual tools

Fig. 4-2. Looks like there's a pot of gold at the end of the rainbow! Miners of the Buena Suerte Mine have indeed struck gold deep in the heart of Oro Mountain.

longer car can operate elsewhere on the layout, but it won't be able to enter the industrial yard or run the Shortline with its tunnels. Cut pads from cork roadbed and install them under the footing of each bridge riser to insure the proper amount of clearance (fig. 4-4). The risers that support the bridges were built to clear track that is not elevated by cork roadbed. A pad made of cork roadbed under the risers compensates for this height discrepancy, allowing the test car to clear with room to spare.

Lay out the Highline Loop temporarily, starting with the ramp of the southwest switch that curves between the Electrical Switch and Industrial Siding Co. and Fuel Depot (shown in fig. 4-5). Use push pins to anchor the pieces as you lay out and align the Highline. At the turnout start with a 1¼" straight section followed by two 9¾"-radius curves and one half 9¾"-radius curve.

After this curved ramp is a span of four bridge sections raised and supported by bridge piers (also known as risers). Inside each pier is a height number. The higher the number, the taller the pier. The risers are

Fig. 4-3. An Atlas 40-foot flatcar with trailers is a perfect height gauge to check the clearance of the Warren truss bridge, which spans the entrance track to the industrial switching yard.

scaled to provide a grade that most engines can climb easily. The risers increase incrementally: no. 9, no. 10, no. 11, and no. 12, ending with a no. 12 and no. 1 combination. Glue a no. 1 riser under the last no. 12 riser, as well as the cork roadbed footing mentioned earlier. This allows the grade to connect at the proper height with the viaduct. Install a bridge and track section between each of the five risers. Coincidentally, Atlas offers four different bridges with track that interconnect to the piers. You may use any combination of the four bridges you like, including one of each. We chose a plate girder bridge succeeded by three Warren truss bridges.

Continue laying track from the bridge span with five 9¾"-radius curved sections to the viaduct crossing. This curve will rise slightly from the last pier to the

Fig. 4-4. A footing pad cut from cork roadbed and a second riser inserted underneath elevate the bridge risers enough to provide clearance for all railroad cars. You need the extra height because of the roadbed under the track.

viaduct because the viaduct is slightly higher than the last bridge section. The last opening in the viaduct must have enough side and height clearance as it crosses the Shortline's straight section (See fig. 4-7). To test this, assemble the viaduct sections and push-pin them in place, using a no. 7 bridge pier as a riser. The riser should fit snugly when pressed into place. A no. 7 bridge pier elevates the viaduct to its final height. The completed

viaduct is spectacular, as shown in fig. 4-6.

Three viaduct sections support three 5" straight sections before entering the other curved ramp. From the last viaduct use one 9¾"-radius curve and a matching 1¼" straight section to the switch. Two more 9¾" curves should connect this ramp to the turnout of the other mainline switch. All that is left is the mining spur. It consists of two 9¾" curves, a half 9¾" curve, a 5" straight section, another half 9¾" curve (going in the opposite direction to the first, thus making a shallow S curve), a 5" straight, and a short 1¼" section. You'll build your own bumper out of ballast and ties. Track always has a certain amount of play in it. If everything aligns you are ready to move to the next step; if not, make the necessary adjustments.

Assuming that the Highline is aligned and pinned in its proper position, draw the outline of the lake underneath the viaduct (fig. 4-7) before disassembling the entire loop. Reassemble the loop on a large sheet of corrugated

Fig. 4-5. Your version of the Highline Loop temporarily mocked up should look similar to this oblique aerial photograph of ours. All connections should align and the rail ends between sections should be flush to one another.

cardboard or foam core and mark along the edge of the ties with a marker. Include an extra ¼" along both sides of the entire loop of track. Draw this edging carefully, because these cardboard ramps will become the roadbed for the elevated track.

Take a Break and Paint

Now is a good time to assemble, paint, and weather the track, viaduct, and bridges. Following the instructions, assemble the viaduct cut-stone support piers. You'll use them at a height of 2½", except for the piers at each end. Cut them off 1¾" from the top by snapping off the bottoms. Then glue the sides together and sand the snapped-off edges square. The piers must be longer in the middle of the viaduct to reach the bottom of the lake. Glue the piers and the three viaduct sections together, creating one long viaduct. The two short piers at the ends go on solid ground. Paint the viaduct, contrasting the stone block against the concrete mortar and brickwork. Then weather it with the ink-and-alcohol wash and drybrush white highlights (fig. 4-6). Set it aside for now, but save all the leftover pieces for other projects around Oro Mountain.

Now turn your attention to painting the bridges. Remove the track from the bridges along with the rest of the track. Paint the Atlas bridges in typical industrial colors: black, silver, gray, or weathered—it's dealer's choice. Weather them, but with little rust—rusty bridges are unsafe. A professional finishing trick is to spray the bridge with Testor's Dullcote and use colored pencils in conjunction with the alcohol weathering wash. A standard no. 2½ graphite pencil looks like

Fig. 4-6. A Canadian National rumbles overhead on the North American Viaduct while the northern lights dance across the sky.

Fig. 4-7. After the Highline Loop, including the viaduct, is in place, outline the edges of the lake with a marker.

Fig. 4-8. Cut out the lake using an X-acto or hobby knife, taking care not to cut through the stringers or braces underneath.

Fig. 4-9. Glue a new lake bottom, using the hot glue gun to seal the edges. Seal the bottom of the lake with hot glue as well to prevent warping when you pour the plaster bottom.

unpainted steel. Rub a pencil over the rivet heads wherever you want that well-worn and used look.

Excavating the Lake

You have a lake to excavate! Cut through the trainboard along the outline of the lake, being careful not to cut through any of the stringers or braces underneath

(fig. 4-8). After the opening is cut, taper the sides to make a sloped embankment.

Using the cutout as a template, cut a new bottom for the lake. Allow an extra inch around the perimeter of the new bottom to provide a gluing surface. You may have to trim the bottom plate here and there to fit it inside the stringers and braces. Once everything fits, glue it in place

with the hot glue gun. Use the glue gun to seal all the edges around the water's banks for plastering (fig. 4-9). Also seal the surface with a thin coat of hot glue, smeared by a putty knife. This will seal the bottom against the wet plaster so it will not warp or collapse. Make sure the edges of the lake shore provide enough room for the end piers of the viaduct (fig. 4-10).

Fig. 4-10. See that there is enough clearance for the viaduct piers to fit next to the shoreline of the lake. Fill in the area between the piers and the track with Sculptamold, then paint and texture it later. Notice the cardboard stacked under the short pier to fill the space between the bottom of pier and the ground.

Fig. 4-11. This is the same oblique photograph as in fig. 4-5, only with all the elevated cardboard ramps installed. These ramps act as the roadbed for the Highline Loop.

Fig. 4-12. An unidentified freight pulls out of the north end Oro
Mountain Tunnel and passes under the North American Lake Viaduct.

Fig. 4-13. The first two cuts on the spare Atlas viaduct section free the cut stone sides for building both Shortline tunnel portals passing under Oro Mountain.

Fig. 4-14. These are the sections left after cutting the side from one arch. Use it to build a compete tunnel portal arch (above the cut pieces).

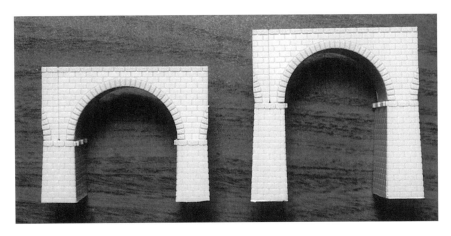

Fig. 4-15. The completed tunnel portals. The shorter of the two is for the south side near the bridge span, and the taller is for the northside portal near the viaduct.

Building the Cardboard Ramps as Roadbed with Risers

Start constructing the track to Oro Mountain by building the ramps, riser supports, and elevated cardboard roadbed for the track. You'll begin where you started before, at the southwest mainline switch. Lay out the first four sections of track for the curved ramp, push-pin the first no. 9 pier in place, and remove the track. Cut out and trim the ramp ends as necessary so they fit in place under the curved track and between the no. 9 riser and the terrain. Measure the heights of the risers and cut them from cardboard as well. Glue the assembly in place using the hot glue gun. Note that on the Oro Mountain Route there is no cork roadbed under the track—the cardboard ramps will act as the roadbed. So the height of the ramp should match the height of all bridges and viaducts. Figure 4-11 shows how the Highline looks with cardboard ramp supports in place under the track.

Reconnect the curved ramp track and temporarily push-pin the pier and bridge span in place. Align the viaduct and push-pin it in place. Now you have established the different track heights between the bridge span and viaduct. Cut out the cardboard for the curved section. Cardboard risers support the cardboard ramp roadbed; measure their height directly from the bottom of the cardboard ramp to the trainboard. By now you have the hang of building the elevated track supports. Complete the job by building the ramp from the mainline switch to the viaduct and finishing with the mine spur. When you've finished, your cardboard ramps and risers should look

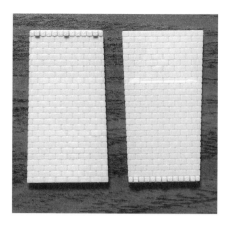

Fig. 4-16. Two leftover pier sections reversed side by side. After cutting the brickwork off the narrow edge, glue the halves together to form a retaining wall.

similar to fig. 4-11. To avoid warping, seal the tops of the cardboard ramps with smeared hot glue, as you did the bottom of the lake.

Tunneling

There is magic in seeing a train disappear from view only to re-appear later on down the track. The idea behind the Shortline Loop was to turn the portion of it under Oro Mountain into a tunnel.

One end of the tunnel is at the beginning of the short half curve just inside the viaduct (fig. 4-12), and the other end is where the Highline track crosses the Shortline near the bridge span (fig. 4-18). Both entrances to the tunnel require portals. Real tunnel portals in their simplest form are just blasted out of the rock that the tunnel goes through. Other portal entrances are made of concrete, wood, stone, or brick. You can construct or purchase any of these if you wish. You can use plaster rock castings or Sculpt-amold to frame the entrances. Later in this section you'll learn how to cast plaster rock faces from molds to use as outcrop-pings around Oro Mountain. If

Fig. 4-17. A Burlington Route diesel pokes its head out of the northside portal while passing in front of the finished vine-encrusted retaining wall.

you want blasted rock tunnel entrances, skip ahead to that sec-tion and complete the prepara-tory work necessary for attaching castings. Provide enough room along the tracks for clearance between the rocks and track.

If you use the leftover viaduct section for both tunnel portals, you not only save some hard-earned dollars, but you achieve visual continuity by having the same brickwork on the viaduct and the tunnel portals. You'll have to cut the viaduct section in several places. It's possible to use a hobby knife, but this is tedious and dangerous because of the curved surfaces. A hobby saw or hacksaw is better. The first two cuts in fig. 4-13 free the viaduct sides from the arched tunnel ceil-ings. Next cut the sides as shown in fig. 4-14 and glue the one brick side wall in place. Fill in the cracks with super glue; eventually

the mountainsides will partially cover the edges of the portal's brickwork. Finish the portals by partially constructing the sections of piers at a 2½" height, as seen in fig. 4-15.

Glue two of the wide pier sec-tions together to create a brick retaining wall between the viaduct and tunnel portal. Re-taining walls are often used to keep the mountainsides from col-lapsing onto the track. Trim off the extra brickwork fascia on both ends and reverse one piece. Sand the matching edges and glue together (fig. 4-16), using a seam brace on the other side if necessary. The finished retaining wall can be seen in fig. 4-17.

Your goal is to create the illu-sion of the tunnel going through a solid mountain, even though the mountain is only a shell over a latticework of cardboard sup-ports. View blocks along the

Fig. 4-18 (left). Extend the tunnel sides along the Shortline track under the mountain. This black matte board will block the view of the mountain's cardboard skeleton.

Fig. 4-19 (above). The north end of the Oro Mountain tunnel with both the train and highway tunnel portals in their proper position. Glue them to the trainboard to secure them in place.

inside walls of the tunnel and curving track will keep those prying eyes from seeing the hollow space under the mountaintop. View blocks can be as simple as black-painted cardboard or as elaborate as cast rock walls.

Make the tunnel walls that you see in the portals from leftover pier pieces, and make the interior walls in the same way as you made the retaining wall. Farther in the tunnel, use black matte board or posterboard as the tunnel walls (fig. 4-18). Once you have finished the tunnel portals and the entrance walls, glue the portals in place as shown in fig. 4-19. The distance between the north portal and the viaduct is the length of the cut stone retaining wall.

We built a set of highway tunnel portals to connect Enville's cross street with the agricultural buildings in the industrial switching yard. You can make them in several different ways, but we used Design Preservation HO modular walls no. 301-13. At the end of each tunnel in fig. 4-19

we glued a mirror and painted the edges black to give the illusion of light at the end of the tunnel. (We could not tunnel all the way through Oro Mountain without running into the Shortline.) We angled the mirror downward on the town side, so a person will not see his or her reflection when looking in from above the depot down the length of the cross street.

Clean the track inside the tunnel very well with a track cleaner bar before applying the hardshell. A track-cleaning car is the only cleaner that will work inside the tunnel once it's finished.

Of Oro Mountain's Majesty

There are as many ways to build a mountain as there are modelers. We've settled on a method that is easy and fast. The entire geologic structure need only be strong enough to support the scenery and a few structures. The hardshell method uses cut cardboard profile patterns covered by

a latticework of cardboard strips for the mountain's contours. The latticework in turn is covered by a thin, hard shell of plaster-soaked torn-up grocery bags. To this shell you attach plaster rock castings from molds, Sculptamold, ground cover, trees, and structures.

The mine. First, take a momentary break and build the mine building. You'll need it to block out the mine area on Oro Mountain. Of the mines available in the marketplace, there are three that will fit easily into the mountainside along the mine spur: Micro Engineering's Poor Boy Mine no. 60002, Model Power's Blue Coal Depot no. 1506, or Campbell Scale Models Idaho Springs Mine no. 48. (There are no surprises in their construction, except that the Campbell Kit is a wooden kit, and we haven't covered those building techniques in this book.)

The Poor Boy Mine is reminiscent of one right off I-10 on the outskirts of Tucson. A vertical-shaft mine like the Poor Boy doesn't look like much—maybe it's seen better days. Then again, it doesn't take much high-quality gold ore to make a mine profitable or to bring a railroad to it. This is the simplest type of mine, in which the ore is dumped directly into waiting ore gondolas.

By building the Poor Boy Mine first, you'll be sure it fits in the available area with enough room left over for rockwork. You can remove it during the sloppy hard-shelling, tracklaying, rock-casting, and plastering. Then, once you've finished all the messy work, glue the base of the mine to an existing cardboard platform on risers and blend in the scenery around it. Figure 4-20 shows the cardboard skeleton of the rock shelf under the mine and the ridges of Oro Mountain around it.

Meanwhile, back at the mountain. Oro Mountain's profiles are patterns cut from cardboard that act as a skeletal frame for the slope. We tapered a rocky ridge from the switch to the mining spur to a summit height of 7", centered over the tunneled Shortline track (fig. 4-21). This is tall enough to dwarf the mine and town without becoming ridiculous when compared to the rest of the layout. Other slope profile sections taper away from the main ridge, creating a three-dimensional skeleton. Between these vertical ridges create a latticework of posterboard strips. This strips can be ½" to 1" wide and as long as you need them. Glue and staple them in place where appropriate. If you do not like a slope or a contour, keep changing it until you do. Remember to leave plenty of room wherever you intend to place rock outcroppings. The mine must still fit into its preassigned area, and the rockwork cannot protrude into the existing buildings or trackwork.

Fig. 4-20. Fit the Poor Boy Mine onto a cardboard rock platform, which will become a rock shelf extending out from the rocky west side of the mountain.

Fig. 4-21. This is the skeleton framework and latticework of Oro Mountain as viewed from the south side. Note how the spine extends along the mine spur tapering down between the lake and the mine spur.

Building the mountain of gold. After setting up the cardboard latticework, you can start on the hardshell skin that will give Oro Mountain its form. First, remove all the Highline track, except the bridge span and viaduct. Glue the bridge and viaduct in place at this time, because you will attach the hardshell to them. Cover all the finished work with plastic garbage bags or a similar material

 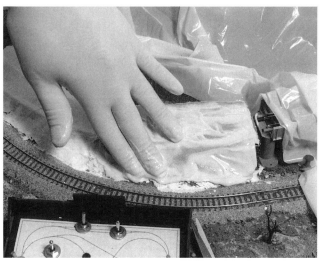

Fig. 4-22. To make hardshell, first drape the cardboard frame, here the berm ramp leading to the bridge span, with damp paper towels to check the contours.

Fig. 4-23. Drape plaster-impregnated pieces of torn grocery sacks over the existing form. They'll become the hardshell when they dry.

Table 4-2
Oro Mountain Building Supplies

- Micro Engineering Poor Boy Mine kit no. 60002 or equivalent
- Cardboard or foam core
- Hot glue gun and glue
- Paper towels
- Grocery sacks torn into palm-size pieces
- Hydrocal plaster and water
- Mixing bowl and spatula
- Sulptamold
- Rock molds
- Rock paint
  india ink and water mix, latex tan and water mix, acrylic white textured spray paint and any additional paints if necessary
- Brushes and bottle sprayers
- Bags to cover and protect the layout
- A little cork roadbed
- Ballast mixture
- Scenery materials including ground cover and reed materials
- Trees
- Casting resin kit and disposable measuring cups and stirrers
- Liquitex iridescent blue acrylic paint
- Tools, including putty knife

to protect it from falling plaster and water.

Assemble the materials in Table 4-2 and you'll get started shaping Oro Mountain. The favorite plaster of model railroaders is Hydrocal. It contains gypsum, and after it sets, it becomes very hard and has great strength. The Woodland Scenics Company offers a version of Hydrocal, and most hobby stores that carry model railroad products carry their line. Virtually any fine grade of commercial plaster will work. Most of us are familiar with plaster of paris, also known as molding or casting plaster. The most important thing about plaster is its freshness. Always check dry plaster before using it. If the plaster has a silky, dusty feel, it is probably fresh. If it clumps or feels grainy and sandy, it is old and not worth using.

The key to using plaster is to mix small quantities. Do not mix more than you can use in a few minutes. Plaster also must be mixed in specific proportions. You cannot rehydrate plaster or extend its life by adding more water—doing so will only

weaken it. Some plasters, such as patching plaster, contain a built-in retarder to extend their setting time. Make an exception to the usual proportions only when you mix a soupy mixture for the lake bottom. You then mix it thinner than usual so that the plaster flows easily.

Mix plaster in a large bowl, always adding plaster to the water and not the other way around. Using cold water will give you a little more working time. Mixing dry plaster and water creates an exothermic or heat-producing reaction as the plaster is rehydrated. It cools as it recrystallizes and hardens. Warm or hot water will only speed the reaction. If you need more setting time, use ice-cold water. Factors such as temperature and relative humidity also affect the setting time. The mixing formula is as follows: pour 1 cup cold water into an expendable mixing bowl and stir in 2 cups dry plaster. Stir until you have the smooth consistency of a cake batter.

You are now ready for the paper toweling. Any paper towel will work, as long as it holds

Fig. 4-24. Once it's dry the hardshell is hard but not indestructible. It awaits surface texturing, rockwork, painting, and ground cover.

Fig. 4-25. The mountain in the preliminary stages of hardshelling. Use damp paper towels to check the contours. Notice the inclusion of crumpled paper towel wads to help form the mountain sides between the ridge spines.

together when impregnated with wet plaster long enough to be placed on the latticework. We have found that the best thing to use for hardshell is small torn-up sections of brown grocery bags. We could not get ordinary paper towels to drape the way we wanted them to. If you do use paper towels in rolls, however, use the extra-strength kind. Industrial-grade paper towels, the kind you find in washroom towel dispensers, also work well. Don't try to use a full sheet of paper towel—tear it into quarters. Prepare a stack of them before mixing the plaster.

Next, cover the latticework with damp paper towels. Dip towel sections into water, wring them out so that they aren't dripping, and cover the section to be hardshelled with them. This preshelling serves several purposes. You actually get to see the contours of your mountain before you use plaster, so if there is a form you do not like you can change it. Moreover, a first skin of paper towels prevents the creation of a huge mess by catching the plaster drips. And finally, the inner layer of toweling binds with the plaster-impregnated layer, creating two layers of hardshell—stronger than just a single layer of hardshell. If the first layer of damp paper towels dries out too much, use a sprayer to mist the toweling with water. This insures a bond between the two layers of paper toweling and the plaster mixture. Be careful not to add to the height of the cardboard

Fig. 4-26. The mountain after draping the grocery bag hardshell. Note the plastic bags covering the rest of the layout, which protect it from dripping plaster and water.

Fig. 4-27. The rockwork supporting the Highline is an example of the results achieved with just hardshell, Sculptamold, and paint.

Fig. 4-28. She'll be steamin' round the mountain when she comes! The pride of Enville churns up a full head of steam as she hunkers down to drag that load around the shoulder of Oro Mountain.

Fig. 4-29. Finish the earthen berm ramp leading from the Indian Bluffs to the bridge span by spraying it with textured spray paint.

ramps with paper towels, and do not let the ramps become soaked, or they will warp and you will spend a lot of time repairing them during tracklaying.

The hardshell steps and plastering the bottom of the lake. Figures 22 to 27 demonstrate the hardshell process step by step. First, cover the ramp or later the latticework with damp paper towels as shown in fig. 4-22. Next, mix the plaster to the proper consistency. Dip the paper towel into the plaster, letting it soak for

a little while, so that it becomes impregnated with the plaster mixture. Lift it out by a corner, allowing it to drain. Drape it over the latticework, smoothing it out with your fingers (fig. 4-23). That's all there is to it! Once Oro Mountain is covered with the wet hardshell, give it a day or so to dry (fig. 4-24). But don't remove the coverings from the layout. You still have to apply rock castings, paint, and ground cover to the mountain, to say nothing of finishing the water features. Figures

25 through 27 show this process on Oro Mountain itself. Sculpt-amold smeared over the hardshell surfaces adds some texture where there will be no rockwork.

While you're working with plaster, you might as well pour the lake bottom and cast some rocks. The Great N-pire train-board should be on a level surface so the lake bottom is level—but check it with a level to be sure. If the lake bottom isn't level, the plaster could run into one end, filling up the lake. Mix the plaster with an extra ⅓ cup of water. This plaster does not have to be strong—it just has to cover the lake bottom, sealing it for the "water." Stir the plaster completely and pour some of it into the lake bed. Using a disposable paintbrush smooth it over the entire bottom, over the hot glue seal, and up the sides of the foam core. Be careful around the viaduct piers. Allow the plaster to dry while the mountain is drying. See fig. 4-41.

Adding Rockwork to Oro Mountain

You should have most of the material for the rockwork left over from previous parts of the book. If you didn't make pine

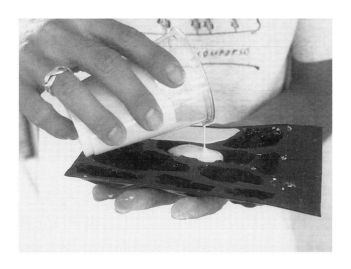

Fig. 4-30. Casting rockwork is easy. Mix Hydrocal plaster to a smooth creamy consistency and pour it into the molds. Once the plaster has set, remove the rocks and install them in place on the hardshell.

Fig. 4-31. Piecing together rock walls from castings is like building a three-dimensional puzzle. Often it is easier to arrange the pieces off the hardshell on a separate board.

trees earlier, now is a good time to put in a stock of them, along with a few aspens or other deciduous trees. You'll use Sculptamold extensively here, so have a good supply of it on hand as well. You don't have to cover the entire mountain with Sculptamold—some of the surface can stay as is, waiting for paint and ground texture. You can even mix some more plaster, apply it, and wait until it starts to set; then carve it, stipple it with an old stiff brush, or texturize it another way.

Start with the curved ramps that lead up and down the Highline. Mix the Sculptamold or plaster according to the directions and apply it down the hardshell embankments and as the beginning of the berm ramps. Continue spreading Sculptamold everywhere on the hardshell except where you will put the rock outcroppings. Paint the Sculptamold with the texturing spray paint that you used in Chapter 1 (fig. 4-29).

Rockwork

If you really want rock faces, nothing can beat the time-honored process of casting rocks in plaster from molds. A number of scenery companies offer rock molds. You can create your own, but that is beyond the scope of this book because it is so time-consuming, not because it is difficult. If you are interested in the technique, Kalmbach Publishing Co. offers several books on scenery that

Fig. 4-32. An application of Sculptamold will act as the mortar to fasten the castings in place.

Fig. 4-33. Push the castings gently into place against the wet Sculptamold mortar. Scoop away any excess that squeezes out around the edge, or shape it into something that looks like more rock.

Fig. 4-34. Painting give the rock castings along the tunnel entrance a lifelike appearance.

Fig. 4-35. Painting plaster rock castings is a simple step-by-step process. First dampen the area to be painted with water from a sprayer.

like building a 3-D jigsaw puzzle (figs. 4-31 through 4-34). Choose an area where a rock outcropping is appropriate and fit the pieces to it. Break or chip them into the required shapes. Try to follow the direction of rock strata and fault lines from casting to casting. Once you have an arrangement (fig. 4-31) apply a coating of Sculptamold mortar to the hardshell (fig. 4-32) and press the pieces in place (fig. 4-33). Scoop away the excess that oozes out around the edges or mold it to resemble rounded rock. This process works better than hot-gluing the castings in place, because you are then left with the problem of disguising the seams and edges. Continue to rock your way across the mountainsides.

Coloring the Rockwork and Finishing Oro Mountain

We tried a new method of spray-painting to color the rock castings in figs. 4-35 through 4-37. It incorporated pump bottles and was finished with dry-brushing. Since the castings are dry and porous and will absorb a lot of pigment, you may have to apply color more than once. Remember, you cannot judge color while it's wet—it will change upon drying. Allow the rock to dry thoroughly between applications.

Spray the rock with clear water to wet it (fig. 4-35), then spray a mixture of ½ teaspoon india ink to 1 pint water. Spray liberally until the wash runs off and the cracks are saturated (fig. 4-36). Next, use the same flat tan latex that you used as earth color, mixed with water in a proportion of 1:3. Spray on enough of the dilute tan mixture to wash some of the black away; let it dry (fig.

include mold-making techniques.

Casting the rocks is no different from the plastering process you've already done. The only difference is that you can use warm water to hasten the setting, if you want to. You'll be able to pull castings from the molds sooner and cast a number of pieces quickly—and you'll need

quite a few pieces. If any of the pieces break or crumble as you remove them from the molds, save them—you'll be surprised where you can use them. Make a few more than you think you will need. Mix Hydrocal to a consistency of creamy butter and pour it into the molds (fig. 4-30).

Applying the rock castings is

4-37). Repeat this procedure until you are satisfied with the results.

After the paint dries, enhance the basic rock color by means of additional applications of the wash or other earth pigments. Use color to indicate the type of rock or the minerals it contains. Alter the rock's hue to harmonize with your ground cover by using warm earth tones—reds, siennas, burnt umber. Or make the rock contrast with the ground by using cold tones—blues, slates, charcoals, or cold grays. You can use acrylics, or you might even try watercolors.

Finish coloring the rockwork by drybrushing with an opaque acrylic white. This is perhaps the most important step. White drybrushing does the reverse of applying black in the cracks—it highlights the edges, which dramatically alters the overall appearance (fig. 4-38).

Adding the Mine and Finishing the Trackwork

Finishing the trackwork is the next step in the sequence. Add insulated rail joiners to all the turnouts of the switches, followed by wire terminal leads. Wire the track through the DPDT switches on the control panel and test it. If everything works, it's time to ballast the track with the same salt-and-pepper mixture you used on the main line. After all, it looks as if it is made up of the talus left over from the mine. Next install the mine with its junk-strewn periphery. Glue the base into the area reserved for it and disguise the edges and seams using the tools, materials, and methods in your scenery arsenal. Zip-texturing and ballasting shouldn't take long. Add the pines and aspen for the final step, then stand back and admire your handiwork!

Fig. 4-36. Next, spray the rock with a dilute ink-and-water mixture—½ teaspoon ink to 1 pint water. Spray liberally until the water runs off.

Fig. 4-37. While the ink-and-water mix is still wet, spray a dilute mixture of one part standard base earth-tan latex and three parts water over the casting. The mixture of black ink and tan will make the castings look like granite.

Fig. 4-38. The final step is drybrushing the rockwork with white acrylic paint. The paint catches the ridges and protuberances of the casting. Drybrushing is as essential to bringing the rockwork to life as the ink washes in the cracks that give it depth.

Fig. 4-39. That Consolidation sure is a busy engine. Here it is caught in a bird's-eye view as it steams its way across the North American Lake Viaduct.

Opening the Floodgates to Let Water into the Lake

It's time to open the floodgates and fill the lake with water. There are two ways to model water in the Great N-pire Railroad. Both methods require painting the bottoms to look as though they have more depth than they really do. To enhance the effect of depth, add rocks, sunken logs, tires, reeds, underwater growth, culverts, fishermen, and anything else you can think of, including swimmers.

The simplest method is to paint one or more layers of gloss varnish or artist's gloss medium. Gloss medium is the same acrylic polymer as matte medium, only it retains a gloss surface finish when dry. Application is simple—

apply to the surface with a paintbrush and allow to dry. You can apply a second or third coat if necessary. The second method is to pour a clear two-part epoxy casting resin into the lake (we'll call this procedure a "pour"). The advantage to casting resin is the depth that it gives. When you look at set resin, it really looks as though you are peering through and into the water. The big disadvantage of casting resin is its expense. The effect is well worth the expense.

Culverts. Drainage culverts are easy to make. All you need is aluminum foil and a ¼" 20 machine bolt. Cut a 1" x 1½" rectangle of aluminum foil. Keeping the dull

Fig. 4-40. Make a drainage culvert by simply wrapping some aluminum foil, dull side out, around a ¼" 20 bolt. Press the foil to make it take on the shape of the threads.

side out, wrap it tightly around the bolt with your fingers, twisting and pressing gently but firmly to shape the aluminum to the threads (fig. 4-40). Now unscrew the foil from the bolt as you would a nut. You now have a scale 4-foot-diameter culvert.

Before you can install the culvert you must decide how you'll make the water. Using varnish will require gluing the culvert along the lake bottom, making it look as if is near the water's surface. All this means is that the water table is down a little. If you are planning to use casting resin, on the other hand, you have to locate the culvert at the actual height of the water surface.

Fig. 4-41. Here is the North American Lake with part of its poured plaster bottom still showing on the left, while the half on the right has been painted the standard earth tan. You may wonder about the name; upon looking down at the lake, we saw that we had unintentionally cut its lower half in the shape of the North American continent.

Fig. 4-42. Paint tan around the shallow edges of the lake bottom, blending in black as the lake becomes deeper towards the middle, and ending in pure black at the deepest part of the lake.

Coincidentally, this is half the thickness of the foam-core tabletop, since the pour will be approximately ¼" deep. In either method, you cut a hole in the foam-core edge and insert the culvert into it. After gluing the culvert in place, use Sculptamold to fill in around it, finishing the shoreline's bank. Figure 4-41 shows the culvert in the lower right corner.

Painting the lake bottom. *Water is not blue,* except when it's deep. Most water looks blue, because its surface reflects the blue sky. Essentially water is clear, but its color derives from the bottom of the stream, lake, or pond, as well as from whatever the water carries in it.

Your challenge is to model the stream's shallows while creating an illusion of depth towards the center of the lake. After the Sculptamold dries, start by painting the plaster bottom and the shoreline banks the base earth color. We used the flat earth tan and flat black for the lake bottom. The color will darken and look wet after the water treatment, so you can use the same tan that you used on the landscape. To attain the look of gradual

depth, mix one part earth tan with one part flat black. Work carefully to blend the transition between the shallow areas near the shoreline and the deeper areas toward the middle. After applying the mixed paint, use a pure flat black near the center, carefully blending this transition as well (fig. 4-42). You might even add turf to the black in the center to look like weedbeds, because when the resin is hardened, you can easily see the bottom.

Now it's time to add some details. Dust fine dirt along the shallows as a sandy bottom. Don't forget to add algae, underwater growth around the submerged bottoms of the viaduct piers. You can submerge rocks, sunken logs, tires, or perhaps a rowboat. We submerged the Wreck of the 97, an engine that jumped the tracks last century and wound up on the bottom. We created it out of spare parts and glued it to the bottom (fig. 4-43). Just make sure you seal the edges as though it is rammed into the bottom. You can place fishermen along the shallows or upside-down divers, allowing their legs to stick out.

Along the shoreline, you can use several different products to represent reeds. Cut twine, coarse hemp, yarn, carpet fibers, or thin broom bristles, push them into a hole, and glue them. Woodland Scenics makes a product called field grass that looks remarkably like tall reeds. Make cattails simply by putting a dab of white glue on the end of a stiff reed and dip it in brown turf mixture. Just remember to use enough glue to seal the holes, or the resin will leak out. Don't forget to landscape the shoreline with dirt and turf before the pour and add an overhanging tree somewhere. Now let everything dry sufficiently before pouring the water.

Fig. 4-43. Put bottom details into the lake like the hulk of the Wreck of the 97, which jumped the track and plunged into the water.

Fig. 4-44. Here is the typical clear casting resin kit. It consists of the part B resin on the left and a part A catalyst, which is added by drops, on the right.

Fig. 4-45. Start pouring in the center and move the stream out toward the edges. Liquid resin has the consistency of syrup, and you'll have to take care to avoid dripping on finished construction. Gently push the resin into the areas with a popsicle stick or tongue depressor.

The pour. A pour isn't that scary, but disasters have been known to happen, mostly because people hurry through the procedure. Casting resin, readily available at hobby shops and art supply stores, is a two-part liquid mix consisting of a resin and a hardener. The resin hardens into a clear plastic that simulates calm water beautifully.

Warning. Casting resins are potentially dangerous. Keep them out of the reach of children. While you're using them, wear protective clothing, use rubber gloves, and wear eye protection. Also, be sure to work in a well-ventilated area to avoid breathing the fumes. We don't suggest using a fan blowing directly across your pour—dust particles adhere to a tacky resin surface—but open windows and circulating air are a must. The fumes are unpleasant and can cause headaches, so pour late at night with adequate ventilation, leave the room, and close the door behind you. The next day you can dissipate the remaining smell with a fan and open windows.

The reaction between the two parts of resin is exothermic, or heat-producing, which can cause problems. To contain the amount of heat, keep pours around ⅛" in depth. If you need a greater depth, use several pours with 24 hours of curing time between them. In fact, if you follow our new technique you'll do three to five pours over a period of a day.

Consider testing your resin. We once had to substitute for a familiar brand. We discovered that we had used too many drops of catalyst, and the first pour cracked and pulled away from the sides. This may have been caused by too much catalyst or too deep an initial pour.

Level the trainboard before beginning the pour and have all your materials ready (fig. 4-44). Resins are self-leveling, and a lake with slanted water looks really weird. Cut off the rounded end of a tongue depressor to a square, and you can scrape the inside of the cup more easily and produce a better mix. Stir and mix the parts well for the recommended time. A thorough mixing is important—an improper mix

Fig. 4-46. Between pours, paint a wash of water and iridescent blue acrylic from the Liquitex company on the resin surface. This layering of resin, paint, and resin produces an extraordinary effect of sunlight reflecting off the surface of water.

can lead to inconsistencies and soft spots after the pour has cured. Pour immediately (fig. 4-45) and move the resin with popsicle sticks into all the areas it should go. If you haven't mixed enough and it begins to set, don't panic—just don't try to add or do anything to it now. A second pour will fix it.

Start the pour in the center and work it out toward the edges. The mix may need help in some areas, but since it is self-leveling, it will flow outward until it finds its own level. Don't try to make waves or ripples—the resin will only level itself again. Work the resin around the reeds, rocks, and pier footings and into the culverts. Bubbles may occur, but surprisingly, they dissipate if you breathe on the surface above them. The carbon dioxide in your breath breaks the surface tension, allowing the bubbles to rise and burst. Watch out for bubbles around anything that is partially or totally submerged.

Now take a deep breath, check the water one last time, clean up your mess, shut the door, and give the water time to set.

Liquitex, an artist's paint manufacturer, has a new line of acrylics called Iridescence. They contain titanium-coated micro particles that are suspended in the paint. Available in a variety of hues, the paint simply sparkles. Dilute blue with water and puddle it over the surface of North American Lake except along the edges, where you'll use green (fig. 4-46). After it dries, pour another layer of resin, coat that, and pour again. As light reflects off the lake the iridescent acrylic sparkles, producing the phenomenon of sky reflection that makes water look blue.

There are still some details to tidy up. Epoxy resins have a

Fig. 4-47. A fisherman has caught his prize catch from North American Lake just in time for dinner as the 5:15 commuter rolls past.

tendency to creep up the sides of the banks. In some areas this is not altogether a bad effect—it looks like wet moss. For the most part, an application of dilute matte medium and a dusting of ground cover will clean up this edge. If you want to create ripples and waves, now is the time to do it. Gloss medium and a paintbrush are all you need. Gloss medium dries clear, and it has enough body to create waves. Simulate rapids around the boulders in the stream by painting streaks in a flow pattern around the rocks with dilute white paint. Let the paint dry

and cover it with gloss medium. It will look like bubbling, churning water. Make lily pads by cutting the tiny leaves from green-colored candytuft and glue them flat on the water's surface near the reeds.

Take care with the water's surface—despite its hardness it scratches easily. If you drop something on it, you'll ding or dent the surface. You can clean it carefully with a soft damp cloth from time to time—dust on the surface of a lake just doesn't look right. You can always apply another coat of gloss medium to give it a fresh glossy surface.

STAGE 5

Details, Details, Details

IS A MODEL RAILROAD ever entirely finished? Not really. There are always more details to add, scenes to create, small structures to build, and weathering to do. Detailing is a great deal of fun. Often details take as much time as the original construction. They are worth the attention because they help turn a toy train into a model railroad. There's no rush to complete any of these projects—add them as you feel inclined to.

The first details fall in the category of additional landscaping. At the beginning of the project you did a quick but effective job of zip-texturing the landscape. Now's the time to return to the countryside and make changes in the landscape.

Consider using Sculptamold to create small mounds, rolling hills, depressions, or small valleys on the remaining flat areas. Make small drainage puddles using three-minute epoxy. Add underbrush, using the same reed materials that you used on the lake's shoreline. This detail alone is worth adding across the countryside. Small shrubs and bushes are most easily represented by small clumps of lichen. This is one of the best uses of lichen, and it's hard to overdo it, as long as you vary the clumps in size and color. A dot of white glue or matte medium will hold them in place. Remember how you flocked the premade pine trees? You can make grass the same way. Flood a small area with

Fig. 5-1. A kite flyer relaxes in the afternoon sun near the industrial switching yard. Randall Laponuke was kind enough to create this kit flyer for us. After choosing a suitable figure, Laponuke scratchbuilt the kite and glued it to a strand of .005" brass wire painted white. Even the smallest breeze moves the kite around.

Fig. 5-2 (left). Here's a headline from the Enville Daily Register: DIVERS FIND ARTIFACTS IN THE WRECK OF THE 97! One of our vignettes is a locomotive buried in the lake bottom near the viaduct. Divers were planted in various pours of epoxy resin so they appear at different depths.

Fig. 5-3 (above). A string of weathered boxcars created by the techniques described in the text moves past the camera in the foreground while a string of unweathered cars climbs the Highline in the background.

dilute matte medium; using a squirt bottle, eject the flocking fibers with a quick squeeze. Most of the particles will stand upright because of the electrostatic charge on the fibers.

Creep mossy vines up the sides of buildings or bridge piers using glue applied with a squeeze bottle. Make a trail of white glue that looks like a vine network and dust it with ground foam turf. If it is a flowering vine or trailing rosebush, add flowers now—or wait until the vine dries and use the hairspray trick. Add moss and clumpy hedges by making a paste of ground foam and undiluted matte medium.

Manmade Details

Unfortunately, humans leave their junk all over our planet, from litter to oil spills. To authentically recreate the world in miniature you need debris. The best place to start is with a favorite among modelers, the junk pile.

You can use anything—leftover parts from kits, lumber, watch and small machine parts, tracklaying supplies, and cast items. Molded junk piles are available, but it is so much more fun to create your own. Make a quick and dirty junk pile by disassembling a section of track and heaping a stack or pile of ties and rusting rails alongside the track.

Industries leave junk everywhere. Among the castings that are readily available to the N scale modeler are 55-gallon oil drums, piles of tires, pallets, crates, boxes, and barrels. Even in the small community of Enville and its surrounding industries you could use hundreds of these castings scattered about. You could even add a locomotive to the bottom of the lake.

Weathering Freight Cars

It doesn't take long for a real railroad car to become a weathered veteran with rust, scratches,

dust, dirt, and grime. Many modelers take pride in how well they can realistically weather railroad cars. However, weathering cars presents a dilemma. There are two schools of thought—those modelers who weather for the realism of it and those who don't. Those who weather their cars do so because everything else on their layout looks used, and a string of shiny railroad cars would look out of place. Those who don't weather are unwilling to mess up the factory paint job on a very expensive model railroad car. Some modelers get around the dilemma by purchasing two cars, one to weather and one to save—but this becomes very expensive. Some spray the model with Dullcote first, so all the weathering can be washed away—but it is doubtful that such a car can be returned to a pristine "collector value" condition.

Model Railroader magazine has published many articles on weathering, and Kalmbach Publishing

Fig. 5-4. We've had fun, but it is time to depart on the 5:15 as she ducks into the tunnel. Adios! It has been our pleasure taking you on a tour of the Great N-pire Railroad, located around the heart of Enville, U.S.A.

Co. has published *Painting and Weathering Railroad Models,* by Jeff Wilson. But we developed our own method of weathering.

First, obtain photographs of real weathered railroad cars to use as references. You can take the photos yourself if you keep a camera handy in the car while you are driving. Often you'll be stopped at a rail crossing waiting on a train or be alongside a set of tracks with a freight passing by. Keep in mind that cars can be weathered just a little or a lot, depending on their age and usage. It's a good idea to vary the style and amount of weathering from car to car. Otherwise they look the same, just weathered.

Next, remove the trucks and couplers. Almost every prototype car has some type of denting. This is the most difficult and dangerous thing you can do to a car to represent heavy usage. Using a soldering iron (on a very low temperature setting) or heated screwdriver, press against the inside of the walls of an old gondola, ore car, or steel boxcar. Heat will deform the plastic outward, making

it look as though the cargo fell against the metal and dented it.

Then use a sharply honed scriber and hobby knife to chip off bits of paint to represent flaking, and scratch horizontally along the sides where car doors slide back and forth.

If you are using more than one of the same car and the manufacturer has not offered different-numbered cars, you could alter the car number. Alter existing numbers with matching white paint or by removing a digit with gentle scraping or fine sanding. Change a digit or entire number by carefully removing the pre-painted numbers and using dry transfers or decals. Sometimes you can give cars a whole new set of numbers by painting over the old numbers and adding a new series. On some cars you can simply obscure the numbers by flaking, smearing, running paint, or grime, mud, or anything else nature might throw at it.

Next comes that old standard, the alcohol wash. The black ink particles will collect in the crevices, cracks, and seams and

around the molded details. If you are going to weather a yellow or white car, use a brown ink wash instead of black. After the ink wash comes a Dullcote spray. This spray actually puts a "tooth" on the model's surface, which will allow colored pencils to adhere to the surface. Additional alcohol washes over the Dullcote will produce the whitish glazing effect that resembles real metal oxidation.

Using a white-colored pencil, you can streak the white lettering that is on most railroad cars. Use rust-colored pencils flat, in streaks, in dots, or abraded around rivets, leaving particles of pencil lead. Accent grab irons with a fine black marker. The secret weapon is the standard graphite pencil—it leaves marks that look like steel. Once you are satisfied with how the car looks, by the way, don't forget about the roof—dust it with a final coat of Dullcote. Compare the same car factory fresh and the one that has seen road wear, as in fig. 5-3.

Finally, add different loads to your rail cars. Junk loads are available for gondolas, coal loads for hoppers. Flatcars are always interesting because they carry just about everything. An old favorite is a hobo or two riding in an empty boxcar with the door open. We have even put cattle inside cattle cars so you see their silhouettes as the cars roll by. Whatever you can imagine was probably out on the rails at one time or another.

We hope you enjoy building your model railroad as much as we enjoyed presenting our model railroad to you. We dedicate it to you and others who have not lost their youthful enthusiasm for one of the greatest hobbies ever, model railroading.

Index